FROM THE GHETTO

The Fiction of Abraham Cahan

Jules Chametzky

The University of Massachusetts Press
Amherst, 1977

Copyright © 1977 by

The University of Massachusetts Press

All rights reserved

Library of Congress Catalog Card Number 76-25047

ISBN 0-87023-225-8

Printed in the United States of America

Designed by Mary Mendell

Cataloging in Publication data appear on the

last printed page of the book.

CONTENTS

ACKNOWLEDGMENTS

I wish to thank Gene Bluestein and Bruce Laurie for reading
parts of the manuscript and helping me with their suggestions
and encouragement. John J. Clayton, Anne Halley, and Sidney
Kaplan criticized the whole, invaluably. I owe a debt to many
students, especially Joe Krausman for his help with "Neshomah
Yeseroh," and Dawn Lander Gherman for making me think hard
about David Levinsky. My debt to Milton Cantor and Moses
Rischin is very great. Fay Zipkowitz of the University of Massachusetts Library was unfailingly helpful. Finally, I want to
thank the University of Massachusetts Graduate School for a
grant that enabled me to acquire some rare materials.

I am grateful to several publications and their editors for
granting me permission to use in the chapters on *Yekl* and *David
Levinsky* parts of articles I have published previously with them.
These are "Focus on Abraham Cahan's *The Rise of David Levin-
sky,* " *American Dreams/American Nightmares,* David Madden,
ed. (Carbondale, Ill.: Southern University Press, 1970) 87–93;
"Notes on the Assimilation of the American-Jewish Writer: Ab-
raham Cahan to Saul Bellow," *Jahrbuch für Amerikastudien,* IX
(Heidelberg, 1964), 173–80; "Our Decentralized Literature: A
Consideration of Regional, Ethnic, Racial and Sexual Factors,"
Jahrbuch für Amerikastudien, XVII (Heidelberg, 1972), 56–72,

and a section of this article published as "Regional Literature and Ethnic Realities," *Antioch Review,* XXXI, 3 (Fall, 1971), 385-96.

This study is dedicated to my parents, Benny and Anna Zweig Chametzky, and to Sidney Kaplan.

Abraham Cahan's lifework was the great Yiddish newspaper, the *Jewish Daily Forward,* which he helped to found in 1897 and of which he was the senior editor from 1903 until his death in 1951. It became the most widely-circulated, read, and influential Yiddish-language newspaper in the United States. Through the pages of the *Forward*—in his own voice, in his introduction of human interest and popular features of mass appeal, indeed, in the very use of an Americanized Yiddish that he encouraged—Cahan played a crucial role in the acculturation of the Jewish immigrant masses. But this important part of Cahan's long career is largely peripheral to my central concern.[1]

That concern is to show Cahan's uniqueness as an outstanding journalist-writer mediating between various sensibilities, languages, cultures—Yiddish-Jewish, American-English, Russian —and his importance as an American-Jewish writer. Cahan's was a complex sensibility, that of an intellectual and writer nurtured by Russian and American culture as well as a Jewish life. His considerable body of literary work, produced between the early 1890s and 1917—the period of Cahan's life that my study rather rigorously concentrates on—deals largely with the themes of acculturation and accommodation seen through, embodied, complicated by this rich mix. Cahan's is, finally, a complex *Jewish* sensibility, standing at the very beginning of the development of a significant American Jewish literature. The imaginative recreation of the effects of immigration stretches in an impressive line of fictional achievement from Cahan through Michael Gold, Henry Roth, Saul Bellow and numerous others. Cahan was a pioneer explorer in the duality of Jewishness and Americanism —a subject that was to occupy every consciously Jewish writer in this century, however various and legion the names—Ludwig Lewisohn, Alfred Kazin, Philip Roth, Isaac Bashevis Singer. Paradoxically, he is an important American writer because in his masterwork, *The Rise of David Levinsky,* he provides a richly articulated treatment of an experience that is a central cultural fact in a nation of immigrants. It is a classic of American literature.

A Note on Cahan's Fiction

Cahan's work included five stories written between 1891 and 1898 collected in a volume called *The Imported Bridegroom and Other Stories* (1898), all in English, although the earliest of them ("A Providential Match") was a translation and re-writing of a story written originally in Yiddish. Six other stories in English were published in leading periodicals between 1899 and 1902. In roughly the same period he wrote a story in Yiddish ("Di Tswei Shidokhim"—"The Two Matches"—1895) and two novellas (*Neshoma Yeseroh,* or "The Transcendent Spirit" in 1900–1901, and *Fanny's Khasonim,* or "Fanny's Suitors," n.d., both published together in a volume in 1913), which have never been translated. More ambitiously, he published in the Yiddish radical press in serial form through 1894 and 1895 his first extended fiction, *Rafael Naarizokh Iz Gevoren a Sozialist* ("Rafael Naarizokh Becomes a Socialist"), revised and expanded in a 1907 version, also still untranslated. He published three novels in English that made him a serious literary figure in his time and and which earn him a place in the history and development of American literature: *Yekl: A Tale of the New York Ghetto* (1896), *The White Terror and the Red: A Novel of Revolutionary Russia* (1905), and *The Rise of David Levinsky* (1917).

The General Importance of Language

Cahan's attempts to achieve a stabilizing attitude towards the American Jewish experience of his time are evident in his experiments with the language and voice of his immigrant characters. This study will focus sharply on matters of language. At first, in early characters—Rouvke Arbel in "A Providential Match," Jake in *Yekl: A Tale of the New York Ghetto,* Asriel Stroon in "The Imported Bridegroom,"—the English language becomes ugly in their utterances, debasing even their mother tongue, evidence of the crude and vulgarizing effect of America upon them. Their language reminds one of Henry Roth's characters in *Call It Sleep*—people of the immigrant generation written about by a writer very close to their experience. The first two characters named above display few or no redeeming qualities preserved from the older culture they came from. Stroon, a slightly later creation, is more interesting and complicated, although finally his fate offers no resolution of an identity problem either. He is vulgarized by America, but upon returning to the Old World, whose values he hoped would redeem his present life, he finds its present reality mean and common, and its past idealized and dead. He does finally extract from the experience some personal satisfaction, but no meaning able to transform either the new or the old world or make him feel less alienated in either.

In the characters of two later stories, Reb Avrom Leib and Reb Eliezer, their world's term "Reb" remains with Eliezer in the title and throughout the fictional world they both inhabit. They speak in their own voices, there is no attempt at Americanization of their idiom or their culture. They are intact, but in some degree artificial creations, almost fossilized forms. Cahan does not employ such a strategy of characterization often, but it is there and anticipates several present writers. Like characters in many stories by Malamud and Isaac Bashevis Singer (whose New Yorkers are often like Cahan himself—of the writing or intellectual class—rather than of the class Cahan usually writes *about*), the Yiddish intonation or *knaytch* (twist, turn) poeticizes the English they speak. This rhetoric re-

moves one from the present: at worst it is merely quaint, but
at its best, it suggests a timeless, mythic reality. Cahan does not,
however, develop in any major way the possibilities inherent in
this rhetorical strategy.

The style of Cahan's final and most successfully Americanized
types—Tzinchadzi in his last story, "Tzinchadzi of the Catskills"
and David Levinsky in the last novel—is utterly flattened out.
They both speak an unexceptional and unmemorable English.
With that instrument, they achieve a kind of emotional deaden-
ing that may be Cahan's final indictment of the acculturation
process. But Cahan does not simplify the matter. Close analysis
suggests that these men were emotionally deficient before they
came to America.

Cahan remains frequently enigmatic, as does the experience
he is representing—at the beginning of a process, the full results
cannot be wholly foreseen. He often perceives the ill effects of
America upon spirit and culture—his story "Circumstances"
shows the numbing and anti-spiritual quality of American conditions upon two Russian intellectuals, while the novel *The
White Terror and the Red* celebrates a luminous idealism among
Russian revolutionaries that would appear to be impossible in
materialistic America. Yet that same Russia that makes America
seem spiritually impoverished is also the seat of a stupid and
vicious anti—Semitism that makes life there impossible for Jews.
Anti-Semitism even infects apparently admirable revolutionaries; in fact, Cahan shows his Russian idealists full of illusions
about many other aspects of history and politics as well. For all
its faults, Cahan's work frequently implies, people can live,
change and grow in America—no small thing.

Cahan is so close to these frequently contradictory facts
and impulses that often the best he can do, I feel, is to name
them—lay them out for our contemplation. That no resolution
of the problems of a people brought within a generation from
an almost medieval existence into the contemporary world was
possible within his own sensibility and time, is evident in the
name of a major novel he planned—*The Chasm*—and in the fact
that it was never completed. An imaginative synthesis of the
effects of their cultural disorientation perhaps required more

distancing from the lacerating aspects of dislocation, and perhaps a more secure Americanism. If so, that would be the task of later generations. Nevertheless, no other immigrant or American, so far as I know, saw the problems in as full a dimension as Cahan did or addressed them with as much integrity and art. Cahan's was an astonishingly intelligent and courageous exploration of a linguistic and cultural process that we see increasingly as a central fact in our pluralistic American life. Therein lies the importance of his literary work, and after an opening chapter devoted to the relevant non-literary parts of his career, the justification of this study and its emphasis.

1860   Born in Podberezy, small village near Vilna, Lithuania.
1880   Member of revolutionary study circle in Vilna.
1881   Graduates from Vilna Teachers' Institute, teaches in provincial town of Velizh. Assassination of Alexander II, Russian Czar.
1882   Leaves Russia with a false passport, arrives in the U.S. on June 6. Gives first Socialist lecture in Yiddish in this country, August 3. Contributes for two years to *Russki Yevrey (The Russian Jew)* in St. Petersburg.
1883   Teaches English in an evening school. Contributes piece in English to *New York World.*
1884   Helps to organize first Jewish union in America, among garment workers.
1884–1886   Publishes short sketches of East Side life for the *New York Sun and Press.*
1885   Begins regular evening school English teaching on the East Side, certified by New York City Board of Education.
1886   Henry George campaign for Mayor of New York. Haymarket Affair. Begins Yiddish weekly with Charles Rayefsky, *Di Neie Tseit* ("The New Era"), which lasts only a few months.

1886–1889 Contributes articles to *The Workmen's Advocate,* English language organ of the Socialist Labor Party (S. L. P.).

1890 Articles, translations, popularizations of science and history in the *Arbeiter Tseitung* (new Yiddish weekly of the S. L. P.).

1891 Delegate to the Second Congress of Second Socialist International in Brussels. Temporary president of the Cloak Makers' union. Publishes first work of fiction, a Yiddish short story, "Mottke Arbel and His Romance."

1891–1894 Editor of the *Arbeiter Tseitung.*

1892 First meeting with William Dean Howells.

1893 Delegate to Third Congress of Second International in Zurich. Meets Engels.

1894 Dreyfus convicted.

1894–1897 Editor of *Di Tsukunft* (monthly organ of Yiddish-speaking section of the Socialist Workers' Party of America).

1895 First published story in English, "A Providential Match," in *Short Story.* Eye operation.

1896 *Yekl: A Tale of the Ghetto,* Cahan's first novel in English.

1897 Founding of the *Jewish Daily Forward.* Cahan editor for eight months.

1897–1901 On the staff of the *Commercial Advertiser,* working for Lincoln Steffens.

1897 Organization of "The Bund" (*Yiddishe Arbeiter Bund*): Jewish Workers' Federation of Russia and Poland, in Vilna. Organization of political Zionism.

1899 Dreyfus pardoned.

1901 Socialist Party of America founded.

1902 Returns to *Forward* as editor for six months.

1903 Kishinev massacre. Cahan returns to *Forward,* in full control.

1905 First Russian Revolution. Anti-Jewish riots in various Russian cities. Publishes *The White Terror and the Red.*

1910 Enthusiastic celebration of Cahan's 50th birthday fills Carnegie Hall.

1912   Visits Europe, meets Jaurès, Lenin.

1913   United Garment Workers' Strike, Cahan plays leading role in controversial settlement. Contributes four-part series to *McClure's Magazine,* entitled "The Autobiography of an American Jew," the basis for *The Rise of David Levinsky* (1917).

1914   Jaurès assassinated. Outbreak of First World War. Meyer London, Socialist congressman from East Side, elected to Congress. The Forward Association the chief power in the International Ladies' Garment Workers' Union. Visits Leo Frank in Georgia jail.

1917   Russian Revolution. *The Rise of David Levinsky,* his last published fictional work.

1924   The Johnson Act, severely restricting immigration. *The Jewish Daily Forward* has a daily readership of a quarter of a million.

1925   Visit to Palestine to see Zionist settlements.

1926   Cahan begins his Autobiography (*Bleter Fun Mein Leben*), which runs to five volumes and is concluded in 1931.

1927   Trip to Russia.

1929   Visits Palestine again after Arab riots, publishes book concerning his two trips.

1933   Roosevelt and the New Deal. Hitler to power in Germany.

1936   With David Dubinsky and Sidney Hillman, founds American Labor Party, supports FDR.

1939   Outbreak of the Second World War.

1946   Suffers stroke; control of *Forward* passes to managing editor.

1951   Dies in August.

CHAPTER ONE

"Socialist—Journalist—Friend of the Ghetto"

The title of this chapter is taken from an interview with Cahan in 1911[1] and it conveys admirably the breadth and significance of the man as he was perceived by his contemporaries. Any discussion of Abraham Cahan's life is complicated by the sheer number of significant matters he was involved with over an unusually long span of time and by the interrelatedness of his various concerns. To do justice to any one part of his career leads one to a consideration of several others: his evolving politics, from youthful revolutionary to moderate socialist, are tied to his Russian past as well as to his developing American experience; his career as a journalist develops in him certain attitudes towards Yiddish, high and low culture, the American scene; his stories and novels draw on all of these. For purposes of analysis and explication these elements will be examined separately, but the burden of this chapter is to provide a better understanding of the whole man behind the work in those years in which he wrote fiction.

The Russian-Jewish Background

Cahan was born on July 6, 1860 in a small village near Vilna, a historic center of several old cultures and a renowned seat of

Jewish learning—Napoleon had dubbed it "the Jerusalem of Lithuania." His grandfather had been a rabbi; his father a teacher of young children, and on occasion a clerk and small businessman. From the age of five, when he moved with his family into the city, Cahan's life, as he was to say later, was largely one of study, reading and writing. He was educated in various Hebrew schools, briefly in Yeshiva, took lessons from his father. His life decisively turned when, largely on his own initiative, he entered a government-sponsored Russian-Jewish folk school that offered instruction in Russian and modern secular subjects. The preparation he received enabled him to enter the Vilna Teachers' Institute in 1877.

This Institute was a cut below the Gymnasium, as Cahan was well aware, but it offered a solid curriculum in standard subjects and certified its graduates as teachers in the Jewish folk schools. Furthermore, it placed Cahan, who had only belatedly discovered the Vilna Public Library (where he hungrily read Russian books) close to other questing spirits who were caught up in the spiritual and intellectual ferment of the period. This ferment was largely pre-Marxian socialist and anarchist in character, and very idealistic. Before he left the Institute as a teacher in 1881, Cahan joined a circle that read and discussed the underground literature of the day—chiefly anarchist tracts and journals, and Chernishevsky's *What Is To Be Done.*

He soon broke with traditional Judaism and became converted to socialism. In Czarist Russia this act was a momentous and transforming one, quite unlike the experience of converts in the western countries. First of all there was the enormous risk; but compensating for that was the sense of an existence lifted quite beyond the ordinary. Cahan compared the experience to a love affair; certainly he felt a lover's passionate and selfless exaltation. On a humble level his transcendent political commitment meant he could emotionally ignore the dismal school barracks he lived in at the time, as well as the misfortune of his crossed eyes (which made him acutely self-conscious). More significantly, the barriers of caste and class, of otherness and difference, that were the birthright of a Russian Jew simply did not exist within the illegal revolutionary circle (actually a study group) into which he was drawn. The image of comradeship, a world of ideal love and friendship he felt he glimpsed there, was to inspire and haunt him the rest of his life (*Education*, 146–47).

Years later Cahan described some of the various events and influences—there was no one single dramatic event—that led to his radicalization. He remembered his mother telling him of the cantor's son who was caught by the police with a note in one of his books, saying "There is no God, and we don't need a Czar." He was reminded of this story again when he encountered injustices from his teachers at the Vilna Institute. Then a forbidden poem, "Who Lives Well in Russia," by Nekrassov, fell into his hands and had an electric effect upon him. He was strongly affected, as well, by a forbidden article on the freeing of a well-known revolutionary by other revolutionaries, which combined thrilling adventure with the highest spirituality. Finally, a poem in an old Russian revolutionary journal that told how three Kings ruled over the world—"Poverty, Capital, the Cross"—made a "deep, deep impression" on him. He became a new man, impossibly idealistic, went around like a young lover. In fact, he said, the idea of socialism he held then was too good for the people around him![2]

Cahan's involvement in revolutionary life and action was actually minimal at this stage of his life—except that in the context of the time, the mere reading of *Land and Freedom* (organ of the anarchist *Narodnaya Volnya*—"The Will of the People"—group) and *What Is To Be Done* were intensely revolutionary acts. After the assassination of Alexander II by a group of anarchists, there was a ruthless repression of all illegal political activity. By then Cahan was doing his first teaching, in the provincial town of Velizh, but the repression threatened to reach him there. The police searched his rooms, examining his books; this combined with the arrest of several of his Vilna comrades convinced him to flee the country. In 1882, he illegally crossed the border into Austria. One life was over and a momentous new phase lay before him.

As was to become increasingly clear, of course, Cahan was taking part in an epic movement of people. The enormous migration of Europeans to America lasted for more than a century,

its last and greatest phase occurring from the 1880's to the clos-
ing of open immigration in 1924. During this last period, the
Jewish people engaged in one of the greatest mass movements
in its own history. Between 1881 and 1910 alone, over one and
one-half million East European Jews arrived in the United
States.[3]

Coming at the very beginning of this great migration, and as a
political exile and intellectual, Cahan found himself in a very
special relationship to the masses. For one thing, on the arduous
path to America, he shared the life of crowds of Jewish immigrants, most of them ordinary folk. At the same time there were
specifically Jewish radical groups on the pilgrimage, off to form
communes in America, that afforded him a special sense of comradeship and mission—he flirted briefly with the idea of joining
one of these communal organizations—within the larger group.
The experience was almost a paradigm of his later career: in
general sharing the fate of the masses, but always with a sense
of difference, specialness, the obligation to lead. Still, it was as
a Russian revolutionary that he saw himself when he landed in
the United States on June 6, 1882, more concerned with the
fate of the Russian martyrs languishing then in Siberian dun-
geons than with anything to do with Jews or Americans. Indeed,
his ideas about America were shadowy at best: not until he saw
a cat moving on the dock was he convinced that the country
even existed in the same world as Russia, Austria, England (*Education*, 217).

Radicalism, Politics and Journalism in the New Land

Cahan's ignorance—and innocence—as he arrived in the new land
was to prove, at least initially, a curse and a blessing. The remote
and exaltedly idealistic notions of the Russian revolutionary
movement of 1881 scarcely equipped a young immigrant intellectual with an ability to understand the intricacies of American
politics, the buffeted but lively American labor movement, the
varieties of American social forms—especially at a point where
these were undergoing change and development in ways that
native participants, emerging from the Gilded Age, were strug-

gling to grasp. Yet in the world of East Side politics, work, radicalism that Cahan and others from Russia were just beginning
to enter and make their own teeming domain, this scarcely mat-
tered. The very assurance derived from a certain narrowness of
vision (though not of ideals) and certainty of moral rightness
enabled Cahan and his fellow Russian-speaking students to
throw themselves with passion—and effect—into the life and
struggles around them. Recent products of emancipation themselves, with all its attendant hopes and strains, they were able,
as Moses Rischin has pointed out, to assume the leadership of
the immigrant community as more traditional guides and sources
of consolation lost their hold upon that uprooted people.[4]

It must be borne in mind, as Irving Howe has observed in his
brilliant study, *World of Our Fathers: The Journey of the East
European Jews to America and the Life They Found and Made*
(a title worth quoting in its fullness, it is so germane to this discussion),[5] that this leadership in the early phase of the "journey"
was basically primitive intellectually and politically untried. For
them radicalism was more often a reaction to orthodox religion
than a real working-class or revolutionary politics—although
they were adept in a strident way in the rhetoric of such a politics. As we saw in Cahan's early conversion to socialism and
his way of regarding it, there was surely an element of messianic
longing in the experience, a hope for self-transcendence and a
world better and broader than the narrow one they had been
born into. At the root was a deep spiritual longing and hunger.
In such an ambience ideas and party designations were frequently embraced in a loose and bewildering way. Those of the generation of pioneer radicals to which Cahan belonged, as Howe
observes, were "a mixture of socialist, anarchist, positivist, village atheist, and enlightened young Jew in love with the heroic
style of the Russian populists." In his autobiography Cahan
describes with equanimity his own enthusiasm in the '80s for
the Tolstoyan anarchist, Comtean and vegetarian William Frey
("a moral giant" he calls him) at the same time that he is willing
to lecture earnestly on Karl Marx to audiences of Jewish workers. Among all the early radicals, and through all the confusion,
however, as Howe justly concludes, "Cahan stands out over-

whelmingly," emerging as "the most lucid intelligence in the early Jewish labor movement."[6] How did that come about for the young, arrogant *naif* stepping off the boat in June, 1882?

In the first place, it depended upon his encountering and relating realistically the Jewish immigrant experience and the American world of work to the radical movement. In the second place Cahan displayed a growing willingness to trust his own perceptions, intelligence and logic in evaluating the meaning of this complex experience. On one level, Cahan simply became fascinated with the American scene around him—a scene in which "a shister (shoemaker) became a mister," and where publications that could earn one a Siberian exile in Russia could be purchased at a corner newsstand, an "America [that] lives more in one day than Russia does in ten" (*Education*, 227, 244). He fell in early with the Russian Jewish intelligentsia and in a significant way that world sustained him; he became a leading figure in it, but almost from the outset he was aware of its limitations.

This is not the place to present a detailed history of the Jewish and non-Jewish labor and socialist movements of the period. As regards the labor movement generally, it will be useful to quote Rischin's succinct formulation of the overall situation that faced Cahan and his contemporaries:

> In the final decades of the nineteenth century organized labor was only beginning to find a means to survive. Varied living standards and craft varieties, added to the antipathies of skilled and unskilled, native and immigrant, made labor cooperation a continual trial. East European Jews shared labor's predicament in the 1880's and 1890's and responded to labor's ideals and enthusiasms. But their segregation in the apparel industries and their individualism placed them on the periphery of labor's triumphs until the close of the first decade of the twentieth century.[7]

Within the historic limits thus depicted, Cahan and his generation played out their roles as the pioneers of the labor movement and a radical press to serve it. In his autobiography Cahan provides a vivid picture of these developments as well as of the anarchist and socialist currents in which he moved. From the wealth of information he provides, one can touch upon some of the most revealing and suggestive aspects.

Unskilled and unused to labor though he was, Cahan was able to get work quickly in a cigar factory, one of the few industries then controlled by Jews and one favored by intellectuals because, though monotonous, the work was relatively light. Samuel Gompers, incidentally, worked on the floor above Cahan, although they did not meet until many years later, when from his base in the cigar union Gompers moved steadily towards creating the leading role of the A.F.L. For a while Cahan worked in a tin plant, another boring but light job. With a small economic foothold secured, he could begin to explore the world of largely foreign-language radicalism that existed in New York. German social democratic and anarchist groups were especially active and in proximity to the Jewish quarters. Almost at once he began reading the German socialist daily the *New Yorker Volks Zeitung*, a journal that he says "played a major role in our intellectual development" with its challenging Marxist interpretations of the news. Within weeks he was trying to learn English from a German-English grammar and exchanging lessons with his landlady's eight-year old child (learning more English, he avers, than teaching Yiddish and Hebrew).

At this time, too, there occurred a dramatic event that illuminates clearly the circles in which Cahan moved and underscores significantly the directions his life was to take. In the month Cahan arrived a bitter strike of Irish and German longshoremen was in progress and an effort had been made to use unaware and recently arrived Jewish immigrants as strikebreakers. When the situation was explained to the immigrants by a young Russian Jew among them they proclaimed their solidarity with the strikers and refused to scab further. The situation impressed the German socialists, who urged the young Russian, Mirovitch, to start a *Propaganda Verein* aimed specifically at the new immigrants (the full title of the organization was Propaganda Society for the Dissemination of Socialist Ideas among Immigrant Jews). The group sponsored meetings, the second of which was eagerly attended by Cahan and his acquaintances—one of whom, with his teacher's gift, Cahan had already proselytized in the shop.

The meeting was addressed in Russian by Sergius Schevitch, co-editor of the *Volks Zeitung* and a dashing figure in the revolutionary movement—partly because his wife had been romantically attached to the greatly admired Ferdinand Lassalle. At the conclusion of the speech, Mirovitch asked for comments and recognized Cahan from the floor. With beating heart Cahan made some impassioned and crowd-pleasing remarks about the need to remember the martyrs still in Russia. Cahan describes the aftermath, which it is worth repeating at length:

> That night Mirovitch and I discussed his propaganda society. He explained that its aim was to spread socialism among the Jewish immigrants.
> "If it is for Jewish immigrants," I asked him, "why are the speeches in Russian and German?
> "What language do you suggest?" he asked derisively. "What Jew doesn't know Russian?"
> "My father," I replied.

Fortunately the situation did not rest with that splendid retort. Cahan proposed that speeches for Jews should be made in Yiddish—a proposal that was regarded as faintly comic. Mirovitch taunted him with the suggestion that he deliver a speech in Yiddish. "Why not?" Cahan replied, and so it was that, "more in jest than in earnest," as he says, the association rented a hall, Cahan printed a handbill in Yiddish which he and a friend distributed in the streets, and "the first socialist speech in Yiddish to be delivered in America" was presented by Abraham Cahan on August 18, 1882 (*Education*, 237).

On this occasion Cahan spoke for two hours on the theory of surplus value, the class struggle, the inevitable coming of socialism—thus demonstrating both the insouciance with which he and others of his autodidactic generation of indefatigable orators and lecturers devoured and disgorged gobs of half-assimilated ideas and, what was probably of greater ultimate significance, the suitability of Yiddish for the transmission of serious thought. He was to repeat his success shortly thereafter and was soon in demand for lectures and speeches as the numbers of immigrants hungry for language, culture, some kind of leader-

ship, began to swell. Between that and language tutoring and
some minor journalism (soon to be described) Cahan was able
to free himself from factory work.

His range of activities and sympathies began to broaden. He
enrolled as a student in a public school (ultimately he went on
to earn a license to teach in an evening high school); along with
William Frey he attended Felix Adler's Ethical Culture lectures
(and then debated Frey from a Marxist position). Still, his sympathies at this time were largely with the German-speaking anarchists—whose leading American figure, Johann Most, came to
this country a year after Cahan. He admired the *Volks Zeitung*,
but its style was too long-winded and Germanic. Later he wished
ruefully that he had paid more attention to it as a way out of
the confusion of anarchism, with its disdain of electoral politics
and a real trade union movement ("How could a revolutionary
talk about such lowly matters," he comments wryly in his
memoirs).

For several years there had been talk of a socialist paper in
Yiddish—a plan that had been discussed as early as 1883, but
nothing came of it. As the Jewish role in the labor movement
grew, the need became keenly felt, finally to be realized when
Cahan and an associate put out a weekly called *Di Neie Tseit*
(The New Era) in 1886. It struggled along for a month, but per-
ished for lack of financial reserve—a reflection, almost, of the
failure at this time to develop labor organizations that could
sustain themselves for more than a period of crisis or strike. By
this time, however, Cahan had become a figure to be reckoned
with in the small world of Jewish radicalism and had, characteristically, also caught the attention of a segment of the English-
speaking world as a journalist operating from a unique vantage
point.

As a way of supplementing his income during his first year
here, Cahan had sent pieces on immigrant life to *Russky Yevrey*,
a Russian weekly devoted to Jewish affairs that had printed dis-
patches of his from his teaching days in Velizh. At the same
time, in his first year he managed to place a piece in the form of
a long letter entitled "The Crowned Criminals" on the front
page of the *New York World* (May 28, 1883) shortly after

Joseph Pulitzer acquired the paper. The letter disputed the newspaper's rosy depiction of the coronation of Alexander III. Cahan obviously had strong views on the subject, as this excerpt from the conclusion shows: "This then is the illustrious family (the Romanovs) which the armed nobles and the ignorant mou- jiks lifted into new glory at Moscow yesterday. Their wild acclaim . . . was a protest against the rights of man, and a declar- ation that people who claim to rule by divine right have the di- vine right to ignore all principle of honor and decency and all traits of morality." The piece had been so heavily edited for its English that Cahan disdained to claim it as wholly his own, but his stamp is unmistakably there.

Most significant to his development in these early formative years was his continued absorption in the variousness and color of American life, an interest fed especially vividly at this time by the spectacle of American politics. Four months after his arrival he was engrossed in a stormy election for the governor- ship of New York, won by Grover Cleveland. He avidly read about the process in the *Volks Zeitung* and the *Herald,* learning enough about American politics to feel that while they may have been "strange, ridiculous, wild, sometimes even disgusting," the anarchists and socialists who argued that there was no more freedom in America than in Russia were indulging in mere talk (*Education,* 282). He followed the presidential election cam- paign of 1884 between Cleveland and Blaine even more closely, reading all the New York papers, attending demonstrations and rallies. It was a particularly bitter and vicious campaign, which Cahan often found vulgar, cheap, nauseatingly hypocritical, but "at the same time, the political turmoil was so interesting and colorful that I willingly succumbed to it" (*Education,* 287).

The practical consequences of all this attention in terms of Cahan's developing career were twofold: he wrote a long ac- count of the political campaign in Russian that was printed in *Viestnik Yevropy* in Petersburg, one of the most prestigious Russian journals (it had originally published the works of Tur- genev), thus enhancing his standing among the Russian contin- gent in America; and he delivered a fiery anarchist speech to a Jewish audience ("The days of the Republicans and the Democrats are numbered," he shouted—adding in his memoirs that "in that entire hall there wasn't a single citizen." *Education,* 289) that came to the attention of John Swinton. Swinton was a native radical and journalist who had recently left Dana's *Sun* in order to begin his own non-sectarian, anti-capitalist weekly, to which Cahan was now invited to contribute a few articles. A short while later he was contributing local color pieces to the *Sun,* itself, and to the *Evening Press.*

So much attention has been paid to these early gropings and directions because in them may be discerned, as we approach the watershed year 1886, the essential lines of his subsequent development. The year 1886 was so crucial to Cahan because in it occurred the Henry George campaign for Mayor of New York as well as the Haymarket Affair and its aftermath. In that year, Cahan's growing disenchantment with the anarchists came to a head and he broke with them for good, joining the Socialist Labor Party. It was a small and largely insignificant party of fewer than 3,000 members, mostly recent immigrants (Germans, with a sprinkling of Poles, Jews, Bohemians, Italians), begun in 1877 and continually beset by problems of direction. Should socialists be involved in politics for the sole purpose of getting votes for a cooperative scheme (the Lassallean view), or disdain that in favor of craft union struggles for wages or hours, or forego both in favor of more direct action? By the time Cahan joined in 1886 the Germans in the S.L.P. had come to the realization that they must lead workers in day-to-day struggles and involve themselves in their unions.[8] It was also the year, as we have seen, in which Cahan first struck out as an editor. Most of his basic ideas and interests were crystallizing.

Despite his anarchist notions, Cahan was caught up in the enthusiasm of the united front of single-taxers and socialists working for George's election. George was defeated, but not by much, and then very possibly through fraud. By the end of the experience, Cahan had been converted to the socialist-inspired idea that the workers would have to enter the field of political as well as economic struggle. As for Haymarket, after the injustice to the Anarchists in Chicago, a wave of militancy and hopes of a revolutionary turn swept over New York radical circles. But these expectations were ill-founded (one is reminded of the expectation of an uprising after the Czar's assassination among Cahan's Vilna comrades). The American working class was far from revolutionary in mood; it had, indeed, to the dismay of Cahan and other radicals, remained largely indifferent to, or even approved of, the execution of Spies, Parsons, Engel, Fischer (*Education,* 326–28). Cahan took the lesson to heart. He read Marx, Engels, Plekhanov against Utopian elites, with whom he now identified the anarchists. By 1888, he was openly scoffing at the New York advocates of immediate and forceful revolution: "Start your revolution on Orchard Street," he said, "and what then? Are there not millions of *other* streets in America? Violence is what we must all avoid. Education is slow; it will take many years. But only so will Socialism come at last in America."[9] The foundation of Cahan's pragmatic and evolutionary view of political change had been laid.

The public struggle with the anarchists for leadership of the Jewish labor movement and masses continued for more than a decade (although the protagonists frequently remained personally friendly) and within the socialist movement there were continual disruptions and disagreements. Two rending issues of the time among socialists were (1) whether the movement should concentrate on winning over native workmen rather than immigrant groups (ironically, Cahan favored the former position in 1889, shortly before, that is, he was to throw himself with his usual energy into Jewish radical journalism) and (2) whether support should be given to Samuel Gompers' efforts to unionize the garment workers within his "non-political" American Federation of Labor or to Daniel DeLeon's effort to continue the domination of the unions by the Socialist Labor Party. By 1893–94 Cahan had allied himself with the forces opposing the doctrinaire DeLeon. Cahan had first met DeLeon during the Henry George campaign, when he had been in Cahan's eyes merely a bourgeois intellectual reformer. He grew to detest De-Leon, almost in direct ratio to their diverging political paths— DeLeon towards what seemed to Cahan greater doctrinal rigidity, Cahan towards a broader if somewhat diluted version of socialist progress.[10]

DeLeon had been recruited into the S.L.P. in 1890 and had taken over its leadership in 1891–92. A brilliant theoretician and strong leader, he imposed consistent and rigorous Marxist positions, eschewing certain kinds of reformism as futile in both the political and economic spheres. He was vituperative against Gompers and other opportunists, as he saw them, within the labor movement, and grossly intolerant of those who differed with him within the socialist party—people like Morris Hillquit and many Jewish socialists, friends of Cahan, involved in the growing Jewish unions.[11]

It is necessary to go back a step now in order to trace another side of this multi-faceted career in which all the elements do finally interrelate. The move towards a crystallized socialist position provided an important impetus and dimension to his work as a journalist and publicist of socialist views. A member of the S.L.P., he wrote regularly—in almost every issue—for three years for *The Workman's Advocate*, the English-language organ of the party. Two of his long articles for that paper were published in 1888 as a party pamphlet entitled *Social Remedies*. He became an important contributor of articles, translations, popularizations of science, history, literature to the *Arbeiter Tseitung.* This journal was the organ of the Yiddish-speaking section of the socialist movement. It began in 1890, and Cahan shortly thereafter was its editor for several years, developing a plain Yiddish style and attitude towards his public that was to be decisive for his later career (about which more later). Leaving the *Arbeiter Tseitung,* he became editor for three years (1894–97), as his literary interests grew, of its new monthly, the literary-scientific journal *Di Tsukunft.* The culmination of all this was the formation of the *Jewish Daily Forward* in 1897 by Cahan, Louis Miller, Morris Hillquit, Joseph Barondess and others in the Jewish labor movement who felt the need for a journal that could speak to the day-to-day concerns of its constituents in a language and with an approach they could understand.

That movement found itself increasingly alienated from Daniel DeLeon, who was in firm control of the Socialist Labor Party and who repudiated the kind of compromise, commitment to small reforms, and responsiveness to the Jewishness of their constituency essential to a real trade-union movement. The tenacious hold upon the people of their religion and customs, for example, had long been derided or ignored by many enlightened radicals and had been a cause of much alienation of these radicals and their views from the masses in the '80s and '90s. Cahan realized early, at first for tactical and later for more rounded philosophical reasons, the importance of these values during a time of intense dislocation, loneliness, desperation. Although an atheist himself, he did not fail to recognize the importance of religion and its rituals and symbols for the average Jewish worker—and indeed tried to use these in a non-abrasive way to inculcate the message of socialism. He felt ever more strongly that at its core socialism was essentially the acting out of a spiritual ideal.

The *Forward* was begun to give voice in its own language to the needs of Jewish unions based largely on the expanding apparel trades now under control of the East European Jews (a process to be definitively described by Cahan in *David Levinsky*) and employing a large proletariat of East European Jews. The Forward Publishing Association, which saw their leadership of the Jewish unions threatened by DeLeon's advocacy of a dual union, envisioned it as a paper with wide popular appeal, free of polemics and abstractions. Cahan was the inevitable choice as its editor because of his experience, his prestige in socialist and union circles, his views. His standing as a socialist in the '90s was so solid that he was sent as an offical delegate from the Jewish section of the movement to the International Socialist Congresses of 1891 and 1893—at the first he created a minor furore by urging a motion denouncing anti-Semitism (defeated), while at the second he met Engels (who praised him for his work on the *Arbeiter Tseitung*). It was equally inevitable that a split with DeLeon and his followers would occur. Within a few months Cahan's efforts to steer a middle course between the S.L.P. leaders and the group of founders of the paper who had been purged by DeLeon from the S.L.P. failed and he was forced to resign. The Association was unwilling to give up the idea of a paper free of party orthodoxy and so in a few years was prepared to offer Cahan complete control of it on his own terms. Meanwhile, however, Cahan, Meyer London, Isaac Hourwich and the others who had been, in their view, "locked out" of the only organized socialist party in America, joined the Social Democracy of America, newly formed by Eugene V. Debs, and the forerunner of the Socialist Party.[12]

A year later Cahan published two popularizations of Marx and of socialism, in Yiddish, but by then he was deep in his duties as a reporter for the New York *Commercial Advertiser*— a journal that enjoyed under Lincoln Steffens' city editorship during the years 1897–1901 a remarkable flowering of talent and intellectual *brio*. One of Steffens' most audacious acts when he left the *Evening Post* for the stodgy *Advertiser* was to ask the fiery Socialist to join the band of writers and intellectuals that he gathered around him—the result was a cultural interaction that left its mark on them all. Moreover, Cahan's first English novel, *Yekl: A Tale of the New York Ghetto,* sponsored and warmly reviewed by the dean of American letters, William Dean Howells, had appeared in 1896, followed by a spate of stories of immigrant life in leading English-language periodicals. In these years Cahan had great hopes for a literary career in English—a subject and a development that will receive more ample treatment later in this study. For the moment, it is important to note that the break with the *Forward* and the Socialist Labor Party was not without its compensations.

Back in 1889, upon the occasion of his first lecture outside of New York, Cahan had realized how little, with all his reading and observation, he really knew America—how much he had been locked in his own "tiny, little world" (*Education*, 414). His experience had broadened immeasurably, to be sure, from that time, but now in the years between 1897 and 1901 it was to receive its definitive expansion and shape. Above all, through his *Advertiser* years and his work as a writer, one senses his relief at escaping the overheated and intense world of Jewish and radical politics. By 1901, when the new and united Socialist Party of America was founded, Cahan seemed quite content to be merely a rank and file socialist, not a political leader—he was much more caught up by then in the possibilities opening to him as a writer of unusual background and insight. Nevertheless, when the editorship of the *Forward* was dangled before him once again, this time with the assurance of "absolute, full control," it apparently tapped needs in him too deep to resist and he returned for good in 1903.

Evolution of Cahan's Distinctive Journalism

In the foregoing sketch we have seen all the elements that Cahan had to draw upon in his distinguished career as editor of that enormously important and influential journal. The editor of the *Jewish Daily Forward* (the name came from the German social-democrat paper *Vorwarts*), Ab. Cahan (as he always signed his name in Yiddish), had been in the socialist movement, a labor organizer, editor and contributor to five Yiddish periodicals, belletrist, and finally, successful journalist and writer for American journals and newspapers. When he returned to the *Forward* he was the generally acknowledged leader of Yiddish journalism, whose voice had to be respected. It will be useful to take a step back and examine Cahan's evolving journalistic philosophy more closely, since it was to have such a fateful effect upon the Jewish community and beyond throughout our century.

Moses Rischin has made out a good case for the seminal role of Cahan's four years between 1897 and 1901 as a reporter on the *Commercial Advertiser*.[13] Cahan had broken significantly from the confines of the world of Yiddish journalism and politics, measurably broadening his sensitivity to the concreteness and nuances of the American reality. He handled numerous assignments of all types for the *Advertiser*—scores of court trials; charity balls and the Fifth Avenue Easter Parade; interviews with foreign visitors and immigrants, wounded soldiers returning from Cuba, President McKinley, General Miles, Prince Kropotkin, and Buffalo Bill (*Bleter*, IV, pp. 102–186).

He learned to respect the techniques of objective reporting, but always, in line with Steffens' direction of the talented young writers gathered around him to seek out "the story behind the story," in the service of human interest and sympathy for the oppressed. This orientation was naturally congenial to

Cahan; Steffens' desire that this sympathy be expressed in broadly humane rather than programmatic terms became in time Cahan's own position.

Ironically, within a few years Steffens and Cahan had exchanged roles in at least one respect: on the *Advertiser,* Steffens had conversed daily with the ardent socialist, but insisted always on steering the conversation away from socialist theory; at a later meeting between the two, however, Cahan was eager to discuss literary matters but Steffens only wanted to discuss socialism. Cahan made several other warm friendships on the newspaper—among his new friends were fellow staff-members Norman and Hutchins Hapgood, Edwin Lefevre, Carl Hovey. Every afternoon when the paper was put to bed, Cahan would lead a discussion group that attended respectfully to this older, experienced journalist, socialist and theorist—who had, after all, already published a novel.[14] Cahan brought the lively "spirit of the East Side" into the City Room of the *Advertiser*, and a knowledge of socialist theory and passionate literary standards to these young intellectuals. As Steffens described it, the office "was a place of constant debate. Any answer ever offered to the question, 'what is art?' was disputed, and hotly, too. This may have been Cahan's influence. He brought the spirit of the East Side into our shop."[15] He also brought some of the shop to the East Side: Steffens, a philo-Semite, loved the cafés, and Cahan was also Hutchins Hapgood's guide and mentor in those explorations that became the basis for Hapgood's beautiful study of the inner life of the district, *The Spirit of the Ghetto.* And Cahan brought some of the liberal spirit of that newspaper back to the *Forward.* Not least, his years with the *Commercial Advertiser* (an extraordinarily productive period for Cahan, during which he published stories and articles as well in several leading American periodicals) lent him a special cachet in the Jewish community—he was someone "who had become a real American whose advice was to be heeded."[16]

Much of this *Advertiser* experience only confirmed or strengthened Cahan in directions already discernible during his earlier career. In his first editorial venture with the *Neie*

Tseit in 1886, he was already sensitive to the response his work evoked in the ordinary reading public. He took the unprecedented step of going out among them personally to question and examine their reactions. This interest in the public's response was more fully developed in his years with the *Arbeiter Tseitung*. Despite the importance of his English journalism experience, in Cahan's own view, his involvement with the *Arbeiter Tseitung* (and not the *Advertiser*) had the most direct effect and influence upon his entire later life (*Bleter,* III, 40).

Because he was rather more interested in English journals than Yiddish ones at the time, Cahan took part only distantly, he says, in the foundation of the *Arbeiter Tseitung* in 1889. But he was quickly and fully drawn into it, since the problem of spreading socialism and general culture among the Jewish masses had always been of interest to him. He was in conflict almost at once with Philip Krantz, the man brought from England to edit the new journal. Cahan thought Krantz's work in English radical journalism had been too theoretical ever to interest the New York public, so he clashed with him over the issue of Krantz's general style and approach. He felt the *Arbeiter Tseitung* should be written in a simple Yiddish, from a Jewish point of view that would speak to the hearts and minds of the masses, not merely to intellectuals. Krantz, he thought, would make a better professor than a journalist (*Bleter*, III, 16–22).

Cahan's influence prevailed, and examples of his innovations, invariably successful with the public, were soon forthcoming. Cahan introduced bold headlines, contributed an article (translated from *Scribner's*) describing African blood rituals, other articles on monkeys, crocodiles, pygmies, the first man electrocuted in the electric chair—in short, items that smacked of sensationalism but did compel the attention of his readers. In the course of time, Cahan also wrote or translated popularizations of Marx and Marxism, natural science, biographies, serials on the assassination of Alexander II, novels by Victor Hugo, Sinkiewicz, and others (*Bleter,* III, 43–47). One of the most interesting features, which he introduced in the first number, was "Der Proletarischker Maggid" ("The Proletarian Preacher")—in which the "Sedra" (the traditional weekly reading of a Bible excerpt) was interpreted from a revolutionary socialist point of view. This feature was a great success, and foreshadowed Cahan's skill at uniting elements of the old culture (such as religious traditions) with the new ideas—a hallmark later of the *Forward.*

Through all of this, we see Cahan deep in "the art of popularizing," as he himself called it. He sought above all to reach the public and in order to do so was willing to simplify (vulgarize and cheapen, his critics maintained) language, thought, ideological purity. The charges of vulgarizing and cheapening were made against him early in his career and would continue, not without justice, through the heyday of the *Forward.* Cahan came to maturity as a journalist, for good or ill, in the world of Pulitzer and Hearst, and learned from them as well as from his own experiences, the techniques of mass-circulation journalism. Above all he had a shrewd and realistic grasp of the condition of his public.

What Cahan aimed for was a newspaper that the simplest Jewish worker or his wife could read—not as a chore, but as a pleasure, when he was at home resting from his work. Cahan knew that his readers were largely unschooled, having been at most to Yiddish elementary schools but untaught in the simplest facts of geography and history known to American schoolchildren. With elitist aplomb, Cahan believed that the people had no real culture to start with, although they did have aspirations. It was the intellectual's function to teach them, sugar-coating the lessons if necessary (*Bleter,* III, 30, 47). "The Jewish artisan (Cahan wrote) was even in the beginning of the 1890's an artisan in the old sense of the word. He spoke the artisan's dialect and hardly understood any other. Many of our workers could barely read unvocalized texts. Not only did we have to teach them in our writings how to think, we also had to teach them how to read our writing."[17] To the charge that he lowered himself to the masses instead of lifting them, his reply would be "If you want to pick a child up from the ground, you first have to bend down to him. If you don't, how will you reach him?" If this sounds patronizing or paternalistic, it is nevertheless undeniably true that Cahan was in closer touch with America's Jewish realities than, say, Philip Krantz or almost any of his contemporaries in Jewish journalism. And the impact he made upon Jewish intellectual life, despite what may seem objectionable in his apparent condescension, was significant and salutary. The testimony of Morris Raphael Cohen, the philosopher who was to become a culture hero for generations of Jewish students at City College eloquently bears this out: "For intellectual stimulus [as a youth on the East Side] I turned every week to the *Arbeiter Tseitung*. In its columns I read translations of Flaubert's *Salammbo*. . . . I was seriously interested in the news of the week and in Abraham Cahan's articles on Socialism, which were in the form of addresses like those of the old Hebrew preachers."[18]

Cahan's even greater success with the *Forward* confirmed him in all his early tendencies. When he came back to it in 1903, it was a financially unstable journal of some 7500 readers. In eight years the circulation rose to 113,000. By 1924, the year of the restriction on immigration, there were one and a half million Jews in New York City, and the circulation of the *Forward* had reached its high point, about a quarter of a million. Its debts were by then paid off, it owned a physical plant worth $200,000, it employed twenty-five writers.

The success was as much due to Cahan's policies and innovations as to the growth in the audience. By 1903, Cahan's views had broadened considerably. When he was interviewed by Ernest Poole (the author of *The Harbor*) in 1911, Cahan said his beliefs at the time could be summed up in this sentence, "If as a Socialist you want to influence real live men you must first become a live man yourself." By "live" I assume he meant immersed in and responsive to the way things actually were. This awareness was to be put to use in the newspaper's basic effort "to depict the struggles of the immigrant masses to adapt themselves to America."[19] But this high-minded purpose was executed in an unremittingly plain style and with a sharp eye for human interest.

Cahan increased the coverage of American news—sex and crime, of course, but also drama criticism of American plays, translations of American writers, interpretations of American institutions. The paper consistently supported demands for better wages and working conditions, although on one famous occasion, in 1913, it was accused of betrayal when it printed a premature announcement of a strike settlement below the workers' demands. Most significant in the success of the paper was the general air of concern for the real problems of the readership—best exemplified in two enormously successful features introduced by Cahan, "The Deserters' Column" (which published descriptions of derelict spouses, an apparently numerous breed among the dislocated immigrants), and, especially, *Bintel Brief* ("A Bundle of Letters"). *Bintel Brief* is worth extensive attention, even now.

It began on January 20, 1906, and is still going. For more than a quarter of a century Cahan took the leading part in this most popular feature ever produced by the *Forward*. Its format was simple: the editor undertook to advise or answer the questions of readers on all sorts of matters, from proper table manners to marital advice and the correct attitude of enlightened socialists towards religious holidays (an increasingly tolerant and sympathetic one). Taken together, the letters and replies provide invaluable documentation of the Americanization process as carried out in the immigrant press. With respect to Cahan, this feature seemed to strike exactly the right note between the needs of the public and his own didactic paternalism. For a realist writer it provided, as well, a fertile field of material. Cahan's willingness to discuss almost any subject of interest to the immigrants led to occasional exasperated outbursts from those who wondered what it all had to do with socialism. One famous issue arose over Cahan's editorializing on the virtues of sending children to school in possession of a fresh handkerchief: when asked what *that* had to do with socialism, Cahan's classic rejoinder was "Socialism has nothing against clean noses!" All in all, as Pollock justly concludes in his detailed and sensitive study, the "mixture of sex, violence, Socialism, education and genuine concern for the Jews of America kept the circulation of the *Forward* steadily rising." [20]

Cahan's interests had in fact been tending more and more towards cultural rather than specifically political matters. Ultimately, his paper was seriously involved in the development of Yiddish literature.

In 1910 Cahan had been justly hailed as "one of the fathers

of the Jewish Socialist press"; some thirty years later he was being celebrated as "the guardian angel of young Jewish writers."[21] As we have seen earlier, the press in which Cahan was the leading figure played a midwife's role in the creation of a Jewish literature in America. Back on the *Arbeiter Tseitung* and *Di Tsukunft* Cahan had tried to educate the public's esthetic sense and to introduce them to good literature. Although he had blind spots and prejudices—he warmly greeted the first play by Jacob Gordin, the finest Yiddish dramatist in America, but his antagonism to him through most of Gordin's career was notorious—he was one of the earliest to recognize the new flourishing of Yiddish culture. Some young writers of talent found a more congenial welcome in the Anarchist press, frequently edited by sensitive poets, but Cahan did publish many little-known as well as a truly impressive number of Jewish writers of the first rank. In 1892 he was the first American publisher of stories by the great I.L. Peretz; subsequently, to name only those familiar to an American audience, the *Forward* published the work of Sholem Aleichem, Sholem Asch (in the midst of great controversy occasioned by Asch's apparent apostasy), I. J. Singer, and his better-known younger brother Isaac Bashevis Singer.

This literary interest flowed logically from Cahan's desire to make his newspaper the disseminator of general ideals of humanity. In Cahan's conception of things literature was the foremost instrument of such dissemination. "Belles-lettres"—as he usually called it—was moral and significant, but not in a doctrinaire sense. True to his Russian origins, he appealed, as he told Ernest Poole in the 1911 interview, for sincerity and "the thrill of truth" in literature, by which he meant the truth about real life, real human relationships and emotions. It is not difficult to see how such a literature serves, at bottom, the same goals as his broadly conceived socialism. For Cahan, the values of socialism had long been "spiritual" and ethical rather than programmatic.

Language and Identity

The views Cahan held could, of course, lead to a manipulatory or demagogic relationship to the public—which some of his contemporaries, not always without justice, accused Cahan of scorn-

ing. Cahan began with a love of Russian culture and strong
aspirations towards American culture; as the years wore on,
however, his identification with the Jewish public of the *Forward* and with the paper itself became almost inseparable
from his own identity. Cahan had been called "nervous and
temperamental" by the Forward Association back in 1897; by
most accounts, his imperious and paternalistic tendencies grew
with the years.[22] Cahan and his wife (he married in 1885) never had children, which may have accentuated his growing ten-
dency to regard his public as in some sense his children. His
phenomenal success as The Editor to whom the *Bintel Brief*
were addressed for help and advice surely encouraged these
feelings in him. He was thoroughly at home in the role of
judge, advisor, Rabbi—and since the public responded warmly,
his proprietary attitudes were reinforced almost daily.

Cahan had taken the plunge towards close identification
with the fate of the immigrants, although he was not then
aware of the implications, as early as 1882, when he did not
disdain to use the Yiddish "jargon" despised by the intelligentsia, to speak to a Jewish audience about socialism. At the
time, Russian was the language of his intellectual self, the
language he thought in, just as at a later date English was the
language he placed his hopes in for a literary career; but he
"loved Yiddish and often fought for it," he says, against
friends who felt contempt for the language. He felt at home
with his Russian-speaking friends, he reports, but he also "felt
a strong attraction to the Yiddish language, more than I had
ever felt in Russia" (*Education*, 281).

Among other things, what Cahan was expressing was the
pull of a developing national identity within the American
context, a phenomenon familiar to many immigrant groups
who had had no such strong identity in Europe. Oscar Handlin has shown how the process worked. Strangers in the land,
recognizing their loneliness, immigrants felt the need to associate with their brothers—a process facilitated by their being
thrown together in ghetto and factory. Ultimately, it was a
common language that was decisive in forming groups and associations—as opposed, say, to a regional identification, which
for some had been the chief form of group identity in the old

country. Many Poles, Lithuanians and Italians, for example, began to identify themselves as part of the nation they left behind only under the impact of American conditions. Religion was an important part of the process, and for Jews greatly so since the Jewish religion is so much more a cultural phenomenon than simply a body of doctrine. Still, language is central in the process I am describing. And of all the institutions established by the various immigrant nationalities to preserve their security as well as interpret the new experience of America to them, the newspaper in the native language was probably the most important. [23]

In the 1880s the Yiddish-language radical press, of which Cahan was an integral part, achieved cultural, social and moral leadership of the Jewish community—with profound effects upon it and upon Jewish culture in America. Regional loyalties and identities yielded ultimately to broader national ones in America (for Jews as well as Italians and Poles), but so, too, did the class and ideological commitments of many radicals. One's theoretical commitment might be to the working class generally, but in practice one identified with a Jewish working class—and for writers in foreign language publications, the ethnic emphasis tended to prevail.

It is not wholly accurate to assert that a Jewish national identity was discovered in the new world. Because of their exclusions from Russian and Polish citizenship, East European Jews almost always had a strong sense of themselves as a distinct people, possessing a "national" consciousness. Even in Western Europe, before the Enlightenment opened the way toward assimilation (or at least equal citizenship), few Jews thought of themselves as, say, Frenchmen or Germans. Nevertheless, important regional identifications were at first imported to the New World. Benevolent associations, an important and ubiquitous institution, were usually based on the town or district of origin (Cahan himself was a member of the Vilna Relief Society in America); there was rivalry between Jews from Eastern Europe and those from Germany; and the differences between Galician Jews and Lithuanian Jews were a staple of folk humor. These distinctions rapidly became inconsequential as Jews from all regions and types came to see themselves as Americans (the wholly assimilated), Jews (the wholly unassimilated), or more typically, American Jews.

A similar phenomenon operated in the ideological sphere. At first the values of most Yiddish writers (there was no distinction between journalism and literature at this period) were almost exclusively cosmopolitan and socialist. But under the impact of many events, chiefly the Dreyfus Affair that began in 1893, the growth of Zionism, continued pogroms in Russia (especially the Kishinev massacre of 1903), the great number of Jews now living in America and able to sustain a Jewish culture—which was destined to become by the 1920s and '30s the most significant expression of Jewish life in the world—a national consciousness, in the form of a celebration of Jewish values, language and culture, came to be the strongest element in the work of all Yiddish, radical cosmopolitan writers. The essential paradox to be grasped is that the press increased and deepened the group consciousness of European Jewry in America at the same time that it Americanized them.[24]

To what extent did Cahan sense and capitalize upon irreversible tendencies in Jewish life in America, and to what extent did he actively create or contribute to them? This may be, finally, an unanswerable conundrum, but the question of the Yiddish language and Cahan's relation to it may be seen as a key to the riddle of who leads whom. At the beginning of his life in this country, Cahan was distressed at the Americanisms that kept coming into Yiddish. They sounded as barbarous to him as those that he later wholeheartedly supported and introduced into his newspaper—the newspaper that language purists saw as an arch-enemy of their cause. Obviously the Yiddishists could not arrest the change in the language. If one asks whether the result would have been significantly different if the *Forward,* the most important newspaper in Yiddish, had dedicated itself to stopping its Americanization, the answer would have to be negative. Without a doubt, if the paper had not adapted its language (among other things) to the realities of American life, the *Forward* would certainly not have been so widely read and had the success it had. Cahan was alert to this fact early and followed it to its conclusion.

Using Cahan as his authority, H.L. Mencken cites in his monumental study of *The American Language* the tremendous impact of American-English upon Yiddish. He writes, quoting Cahan, "The Americanisms absorbed by the Yiddish of this country have come to stay. To hear one say 'Ich hob a *billet* fur heitige vorschtellung' [instead of, presumably, 'Ich hob a ticket for today's show'] would be as jarring to the average East Side woman, no matter how illiterate and ignorant she might be, as the intrusion of a bit of Chinese in her daily speech."[25] The truth of this observation seems to me unarguable. One has to conclude that Americanization of the language and the people would have occurred with or without Cahan and the *Forward*. One feels that both his enemies and his friends claim too much for him. The forces working towards the Jews' Americanization, as with almost all immigrant groups, were simply and finally irresistible.

Cahan occupied a unique position among his peers. In attempting to embrace the contradictions within his life he was responding to and embodying fundamental realities of the American Jewish experience. In religious and cultural as well as political matters he seems consistently to be struggling against right and left tendencies. To orthodox Jews or, in the question of language and related cultural matters, the Yiddishists, Cahan and his influence might represent the worst of secularizing Americanism; but among "allrightniks"—the name Cahan coined to designate those middle-class, upwardly aspiring Jews who often played down their Jewishness—his concern with Yiddish and the downtown masses would be anathema. Cahan attacked each end of the spectrum within the Jewish community, but of course took something from each view. To his critics he could seem callow and opportunistic; more sympathetically, he can be seen as mediating a difficult synthesis. In this sense, we can better understand his great importance as a culture figure and symbol—as Nathan Glazer has said, "If one had to select a single person to stand for East European Jews in America, it would be Abraham Cahan."[26]

In 1895 Cahan underwent a simple operation that straightened out his lifelong strobism. The operation had almost a symbolic quality; his vision was now relieved of distortion, just before the period of his most active mediation between the American and Jewish worlds. His chief task soon became that of interpreting the reality of American life for his Jewish readers. At the same time he often assumed the role of Russian intellectual or expert on Jewish affairs among his *Advertiser* colleagues. Moreover, there were American journals that solicited his views of Russian revolutionary activities, or the impact of the Dreyfus affair on the Jewish community.[27] Cahan was able to gauge his audiences and to be a lucid interpreter of unknown areas of life and thought for them. This ability was probably his greatest contribution as a journalist, similar to the gifts he brought to the writing of imaginative literature.

CHAPTER TWO

Development of a Realist: "The Thrill of Truth"

In the Mainstream of American Literary Realism

In literary matters Cahan was from first to last a Realist.[1] As
such he was in the vanguard among the better writers of his day
—as Howells was so generously to observe of him. The term
"Realism" has of course been defined variously, but it is necessary at the beginning of this discussion to establish some, at
least, of its essential meanings and history.

The term first appeared in France in 1826, where it was used
to describe a literary method of imitating originals from nature
as opposed to the neo-classic method of imitation from art. As
an approach to writing it triumphed in the work of Balzac,
Stendhal, Flaubert, from which it received the immense authority it enjoys to this day. In England, as well, the method of
fidelity and verisimilitude to detail in scene and character portrayal, as well as to probability of situation and manners, informed the great line of nineteenth century fiction—the work
of Jane Austen, George Eliot, George Meredith, Thackeray,
Trollope. The conception of what "reality" was varied with
writers, of course—was it to be found only in ordinary and commonplace things, in average lives and events, as some Realists
maintained, or was it to be seen as great underlying truths best
grasped in heightened moments and lives? Despite such different
emphases, the central principle of holding up fictional presenta-

tion to the test of plausible behavior of living men and women—
which went along, as well, with a growing awareness everywhere
of the importance of science, technology, fact—clearly prevailed
over any standards of romance and ideality.

The principles of realistic art and writing were debated in
Europe long before they emerged in America, although they
were known here in the readily available work of the Europeans
and were part of the cosmopolitan tastes of those who were to
be in the forefront of American Realism. That movement began
in earnest in America after 1865, fed by native traditions of
western humor, folklore, local color writing, and, of course,
that crucible of unromantic experience, the Civil War. The leading exponents of Realism in America were DeForest, Twain,
Howells, James. Their definitions of this literary approach varied, but they all held up honesty to life, in one way or another,
as the standard against which literary performance was to be
measured.

By the time of the '90s, Realism was to some degree an em-
battled position in American literary affairs. In that decade even
such celebrated writers as Howells, James and Twain were to
feel, as Ziff cogently observes, "the continuity of their careers
. . . interrupted."[2] On the one hand, they felt estranged by the
movement towards Naturalism—that excessive form of Realism
exemplified in France by the work of Zola and here in the early
novels of Stephen Crane, in which there was a concentration on
the lower elements of existence, presented deterministically and
pessimistically. On the other side, there was the last-ditch stand
of Romance and the reaction of "ideality" to "sordid" reality that
filled many of the leading magazines. In pursuit of an audience he
felt he had lost in the early '90s, James abandoned the writing
of fiction in order to write plays (which were disastrously received). Twain's pessimism in the period, a combination of personal, commercial and philosophical disillusion, is well-known.
Howells' response as an editor and critic was to champion the
work of younger writers, when he could, who continued the
fight for Realism. Cahan was one of these younger Realists—
along with Hamlin Garland, Crane (Howells was not put off
by his naturalistic tendencies), Paul Lawrence Dunbar, Charles
Chesnutt.

Social Conditions in the 1890s and the Popular Literary Response

The period in which Cahan began his literary career was one of great social and economic change, contradiction, distress. The face of America had begun to assume its unmistakably modern form: the end of the frontier and the agrarian dream, a triumphant technology and mechanization, powerful corporate capitalism in arrogant dominion at home and abroad, above all the growth of great cities and attendant urban problems. Statistics will tell part of the tale. Six million immigrants arrived in America between 1870 and 1890; in 1890 America was the leading producer of iron and steel in the world, and the leading manufacturing nation; New York had grown from 1½ million in 1870 to 2½ million in 1890; Chicago from 28,000 in 1850 to 300,000 in 1870, to 1 million in 1890. There had been three millionaires in 1861; there were 3,800 by 1900. Among the new inventions were the Bessemer steel process, oil refining and gas illumination, the steam turbine, incandescent lamp, telephone, refrigerator, typewriter, and phonograph.[3] But these are only lists and statistics. Some of the human costs of this growth and change were recorded by Jacob Riis in *How the Other Half Lives,* his 1890 study of slum conditions. Here he describes a sweat shop in "Jewtown" in New York:

> Two young girls, not fifteen, and a boy who says unasked that he is fifteen and lies saying it, are at the machines sewing knickerbockers, "knee-pants" in the Ludlow Street dialect. The floor is littered ankle-deep with half-sewn garments. In the alcove, on a couch of many dozen of "pants" ready for the finisher, a bare-legged baby with pinched face is asleep. A fence of piled-up clothing keeps him from rolling off on the floor. . . .
>
> Pickles are favorite food in Jewtown. They are filling and keep the children from crying with hunger. Those who have stomachs like ostriches thrive in spite of them and grow strong—plain proof that they are good to eat. The rest? "Well, they die," says our guide, dryly.[4]

Riis goes on to describe the effects of pauperism in New York upon girls, children, older people, in the streets, in prisons, almshouses and insane asylums. A grim and graphic picture. One telling statistic is that one of every ten persons dying in the city was buried in potter's field. The same sort of graphic testimony to the inhumanity of the prevalent social arrangements was made in Robert Hunter's classic study, *Poverty* (1904) and in John Spargo's *The Bitter Cry of the Children* (1906).[5] Both estimated that the poor in America in 1904 numbered at least ten million out of a population of 82 million. Spargo focused upon the effects of poverty on children, showing how many were blighted in growth, or died prematurely through defects of diet and care due to poverty. He was most powerful in his depiction of child labor, which easily exceeded the official figure of 1.7 million employed in mine, mill and shop.

The huge ghettoes of poor and, in this period, of ethnically varied (and seemingly unassimilable) populations, were becoming visible to the middle-class—partly through such books and studies as those above—which often led to a feeling of threat and dislocation by that class. A reading public drawn from a class whose values and assumptions might be threatened by too severe an exposure to such grim social realities could not be expected to respond to work that was not basically reassuring. The great popularity of Charles M. Sheldon's *In His Steps* is a case in point. On the surface it is a novel that touched on the prevailing social issues (asking what Jesus would do if faced with them), but which left intact the complacent values of a white, middle-class, Protestant and Anglo-Saxon public.[6] That public did not display a great desire to confront seriously the disturbing realities of American life in the fiction they favored.

The prevailing mood was one of escape. "Towards the end of the century," writes the literary historian James D. Hart, "the romance became almost synonomous with the novel in the public mind and was the most popular form of reading matter." It is important to note that in 1892, the year Cahan published his first story, the book most widely read by the American public was Francis Marion Crawford's historical romance, *Don Orsino*, and that in 1913, the year Cahan serialized "The Autobiography of an American Jew" (the basis of his realistic masterpiece, *The Rise of David Levinsky*), the American public had made best-sellers of *Laddie* and *Pollyanna*.[7] Leaving aside questions of popular taste, what is more appalling is that during this period such books as these, as well as *The Virginian, David Harum, Mrs. Wiggs of the Cabbage Patch* were treated as serious literature by critics in respected journals. Romance and sentiment became reactions to conflict and complexity in the society, identifiable with the waning energies of the genteel tradition.[8]

The realistic spirit and its later development in Naturalism was to become associated for a time with the sordid, the sensational and degraded, the inelegant and the unartistic. "The more reality the better! But let it be reality all the way through; reality of the spirit as well as of the flesh, not a grovelling reality which ignores the 'Romantic spirit,' " said Richard Watson Gilder in the late '80s. Gilder became the influential editor of the *Century* in the 1890s; his views were similar to those of the unsympathetic readers Cahan encountered when his first English novel was being sent around to potential publishers. Realism was a fine thing, as long as it was romantic.[9]

Radical and Journalistic Contributions to Cahan's Realism

Cahan was not wholly unaffected by the conventions of popular fiction—a few of his stories (as he later admitted) are flawed by them, and parts of the *The White Terror and the Red* (as I will show in a later chapter) suffer from a certain genteel ideality in sections dealing with the relations of men and women that are absent from his best work. But the bulk of his work must be seen as being in conscious opposition to such effusions as Gilder's. In his fiction, Cahan was to become increasingly concerned with the realities of the spirit, but he always saw these as inevitably tied to the realities of social life, the flesh, and credible human circumstance. Although his ghetto tales do not dwell on exposing conditions such as those revealed in Riis's work, Cahan was always concerned with the world of verifiable fact and a plausible, rationalistic view of society and man. At his best he practiced a shrewd, sensitive, critical Realism. The sources of that Realism were various, although they derive from a central core of values.

As a socialist intellectual, he was committed to raising the consciousness of all aspects of reality in himself, his comrades, his followers. Mystification and obscurantism were almost by definition in the service of oppression—the task of socialists was to provide a clear view of the actual workings of society. The unvarnished truth was to be the basis of political action. As Cahan matured, the truth was seen less and less to be embodied in slogans and dogma; complication and complexity were inevitably part of a realistic vision of life.

In his years as a radical editor he pursued his enlightening task in two chief ways—by direct exhortation and analysis, and by translating classics of thought and literature that contributed to a clear understanding of human behavior in society. In the decade of the '90s he was greatly interested in sociology and anthropology, undertaking an ambitious program of translating Marx, Darwin, Herbert Spencer in *Di Tsukunft* (which was more of a little magazine than a newspaper). In addition, and with increasing emphasis, he came to value greatly the moral and social importance of literature. This high valuation he owed chiefly to his Russian origins. In Russia, a society which had no free press, parliament, or other democratic institutions through which important issues of the day could be discussed freely, intellectuals and the enlightened classes looked toward the stage and the novel for direction—that is, they looked for the very opposite of romantic escape in their literature. Cahan maintained this conception from the beginning to the end of his career. In the 1890s, as he turned from his purely political concerns towards literature, he translated Tolstoy's *The Kreutzer Sonata,* Howells' *A Traveler From Altruria,* a story by Thomas Hardy, and many other works that provided his Jewish readers more sophisticated and mature views of sex, marriage, and society than were available to the general American reading public.

It will be recalled that Cahan learned much about American life and about objective reporting during his years as an *Advertiser* reporter. Many of the things he wrote for the English-language press in the '80s and '90s contributed to his more formal work as a writer of realistic fiction. As early as 1888, he contributed stories and sketches to the *New York Sun* (edited by

Charles A. Dana) and the *Post*. Despite the occasional sentimentality of their "human interest" slant, many of these may be looked upon as training for realistic fiction. One piece, "Hebrews in Summer Hotels—How They Are Treated—a Strange but Strictly True Illustration" (*New York Sun,* September 2, 1888), can still be read pleasurably. It is an illuminating, lively, and somewhat wry account of the practice of discrimination against Jews in summer resort hotels, and the practice adopted by some Jews of using "summer names" (i.e., Anglo-Saxon ones) in order to get hotel reservations. Ten years later he wrote a piece called "Imagined America—How a Young Russian Pictured It." It is excellently written, sophisticated, and contains images that reappear in much of his work (as these sub-headings indicate: "A many-colored meadow with tall, young beardless men in Gray Overcoats—Women Had Been Forgotten—The Language—The Twittering of Birds Trying to Speak French—The Immigrant's Discovery—A Live Cat, a Blue-Coated Customs Official and a Frog-like Preacher with a Bandaged Hand."). Another piece of that later period (July 9, 1898) is called "Mother of Immigrants—Unofficial Function of the Barge Office Matron," which includes the story of a bride wooed by mail, a debate about it in the barge office, and the matron's help in happily resolving the problem. The material thus worked up for a newspaper sketch was the basis for two stories he wrote shortly thereafter ("A Marriage by Proxy," and "Dumitru and Sigrid").

Notwithstanding the importance of his *Advertiser* years, his experience as a Yiddish journalist—especially on the *Arbeiter Tseitung*—undoubtedly exerted a greater influence upon his entire later life (as he himself claimed in *Bleter,* III, 4). In his first year as editor of the *Arbeiter Tseitung,* the creation of *Der Proletarshker Maggid* series forced Cahan into imaginative and literary directions. Faced with the weekly task of providing a class-conscious, proletarian interpretation of a Biblical episode——Joseph and his brothers, or Moses protecting a Jewish worker from an overseer—Cahan had to let himself go imaginatively, sketch a scene vividly for his readers, rearrange the material, draw an appropriate moral. In fact it was in this column that Cahan began his first proper story, "Mottke Arbel and His Ro-

mance," and ran it there for five issues. His first extended fiction, *Rafael Naarizokh* was also serialized in these same pages a
few years later. He did, as well, a popular regular series, beginning in May, 1895, called "Fun a Vort a Kvort"("From a Word
a Quart") that bears significantly on his development as a writer.
In the guise of "The Hester Street Reporter" he allowed himself, as he described it, "half-belletristic thoughts and expressions" upon peoples' lives or minor incidents in those lives (sam-
ple titles: "An Ice-Box," "Misfit," "Cats," "Again Cats")
(*Bleter*, III, 409).

Realism in Cahan's Theoretical and Practical Criticism

Cahan was also trying to work out, in English and Yiddish, his
theoretical and critical position as a Realist. First, in English, he
wrote a lengthy and ambitious theoretical piece called "Realism," which appeared in *The Workmen's Advocate* in 1889.
Thereafter, in the early '90s, he made several contributions to
the subject in reviews of plays and fiction in the *Arbeiter
Tseitung*. His conception of art was being shaped by his reading
of Howells and James in the '80s (in a debating club he had
joined, he was surprised to learn how few members—all American college men—had read anything at all by these two contemporary masters), and especially of Tolstoy, who was then
being issued in English translation and was becoming known to
a more general American audience.

The immediate occasion of "Realism" had been an exhibit in
New York in 1888 of the Russian painter Vereschagin. The exhibit featured the artist's pictures of the Russian-Turkish war of
1877. The realistic scenes of suffering, the portraits of simple
and unheroic soldiers, made a great impression upon Cahan and
his wife, who had spent their last few dollars in order to twice
attend the exhibition. Cahan was annoyed by the critics who
praised Vereschagin's talent but decried his subject—pictures of
pain, they maintained, could not be pleasurable. The essay on
"Realism" was conceived as a philosophical effort to combat
that view theoretically.

Cahan himself called it "a philosophical consideration of the nature of art" (*Education,* 404). First delivered as a lecture for the Socialist Labor Party, "it presents its arguments," as Sanders cogently observes, "in the excessively lofty tones of a man who clearly feels he must struggle to prove his right to talk on such a subject." Nevertheless, as Sanders says, the piece does contain "touches of fairly sophisticated argument"[10] as well as the basic outline of Cahan's enduring version of Realism.

In the essay, Cahan maintains that art flows from man's imitative nature, although he tries to avoid thinking of Realism as mere photographic reproduction of the world of nature. He gropes towards a conception of sensation as a form of knowledge, so that "the end of imitative activity is not so much to copy the outside nature as to stimulate the sensations which it evokes in us." [11] Unfortunately, this idea is only half-developed —and in a sense, only half-believed—by Cahan, whose other utterances on the subject, in this essay and certainly elsewhere, suggest a predisposition towards some form of photographic Realism in the arts. The real center of Cahan's concern is the "thrill of truth" to be discovered in a faithful representation of the world as it is.

Cahan specifically praises Tolstoy, "The greatest of Realists, [who] affords us more pleasure by the pedantic truthfulness and impartiality to nature than any of the polished and sifted novels which are especially devoted to the delight of the reader." The praise of "pedantic truthfulness" is perhaps revealing of Cahan's instinctive predelictions, undercutting many of the high-flown philosophical theories that open the essay, but considering that it is being said of Tolstoy, it is not as narrow-minded as it may at first glance seem. Cahan concludes his essay with compliments to William Dean Howells who, although no socialist, by his vision as a Realist must, Cahan thought, write so honestly about life as to necessarily attack the present system based on inequality and injustice. It seemed inescapable to Cahan that literary Realism and socialism must ultimately work towards the same end.[12]

While working on his autobiography, Cahan re-read the piece

and emphasized what he considered its main argument: that the power of realistic art arose from "the pleasure we derive from recognizing the truth as it is mirrored in art" (*Education,* 405). In an era of extreme aestheticism, in which "the beautiful" was likely to be defined in quasi-sentimental and complacently bourgeois terms, Cahan had asserted, in effect, that beauty lay in truth. Of course the truth as he saw it lay in a scientific socialist view of society and a view of human personality displayed in the great Realist novels. "It is truth that we admire and that is the source of our artistic delight. The heart experiences a thrill in recognizing a friend in a faithful portrait," he wrote in summarizing the essay for his autobiography. "But capitalist critics don't want the truth. It disturbs the class they serve" (*Education,* 405). Even in the 1920s Cahan did not repudiate these views, although he said he would now put them less propagandistically.

In his practical criticism in the Yiddish press Cahan encouraged work that was true to people's speech and action, faithful to real lives, unidealized and unexpurgated. He set himself against the debased popular taste in the Yiddish theater of the day and tried to raise the literary level of his reading public. In his first attempt at drama criticism, a significant review of *Siberia,* a play by Jacob Gordin, Cahan highly praised the play's truth to the speech and life of real people. Historical and sensational melodramas had held the stage until then and Cahan heralded this production as the beginning of "a new chapter of the Jewish theater" (*Bleter,* III, 188). Since their newspapers and their theater were the two most important educational influences upon the Jewish people, it was logical for the socialist and Realist journalist Cahan to proselytize for his aesthetic conceptions on the stage.

The play's story line was extremely simple. A Jew is sent to Siberia for some crime. He escapes. He lives under a false name in a Jewish village where he achieves a good business, a nice house, fine friends, good teachers for his children. A fellow Jew betrays his secret identity. The play ends as the unfortunate man says goodbye to his family and friends is taken back to Siberia. What Cahan thought made such an unpretentious drama noteworthy was that it was true to life. Its actors spoke a simple Yiddish—the speech of living people (who never spoke the affected Germanicized Yiddish that was popular on the stage.) No one in the cast shrieked, was overtly theatrical, false, or mannered. The leading actress spoke like a real Jewish girl from a Russian village. Realism was there on the stage, Cahan observed; he congratulated the effort by Gordin and the producer (Jacob Adler) to create a "true" theatre. That kind of theater, he said, would speak to the noblest part of the Jewish spirit, reaching the heart of even the uncultivated Jew with stronger words than sensational false pieces with sensational language. The play *Siberia*, he concluded, should be warmly greeted. In his autobiography, Cahan tied in the basic assumptions of this review with his "Realism" article—especially with his view that the essence of aesthetic pleasure lay in the pleasure of recognition (*Bleter,* III, 192–93).

A few months later, in a more ambitious if occasionally slapdash piece called "The Yiddish Theater and American Novels," (*Arbeiter Tseitung,* April 29, 1892), Cahan makes some shrewd observations on the state of American literary culture. Although he had written only one Yiddish story at the time, he seemed to be laying the groundwork for his own literary efforts in English.

He maintained in the article that with the production of *Siberia* the Jewish theater had indeed matured, yet one still left the theaters hungry for more life-like scenes and portrayals. The Jewish theater still needed better material than the broad slapstick farce that largely predominated on the stage. "We make comparisons between the Jewish and American stage," he writes, "but in order to make ourselves feel superior, we tend to use their Irish Bowery variety show as the standard." In fact, however, that is not the true American type. "True American literature is very interesting," Cahan declares (but then without elaboration begins to speak of its deficiencies). "The trouble with our Yiddish stage is that it is too dirty, which theirs is not. The trouble with their stage is that it is too pious and moralizing. Americans," Cahan says, "are too smug about their rectitude. If they were to translate Tolstoy, word for word, it would be considered by the Americans unfit for family entertainment.

True literature mirrors life—including relations between men and women. If we don't put in the dark parts along with the light, the portrait emerges pale and dead. Thackeray laughs at false modesty; American literature is full of it. The French are proceeding to reveal the truth of things [about sex and class-warfare, that is]. American literature and Yiddish theater," the article concludes, "could both improve in the direction of Realism."

Tolstoy's presence is evoked again and again in this period of Cahan's restless turning from politics and from social theory (he had been planning a study of Darwin and Spencer, *Bleter*, IV, 20). One sees that his relation to Tolstoy's work, in a sense, provides a measure of his own change and growth. It would appear, paradoxically, that his experience in America enabled him better to appreciate the Russian master. As he tells it in his autobiography, he had read *Anna Karenina* for the first time in Vilna in 1881—because everyone was reading the book—but he confesses that it did very little for him. Thereafter, his wife Anya, who was an intellectual of the purest kind, kept him abreast of all the Russian writers, whom she read avidly. She told him of Turgenev, Pushkin, and especially Tolstoy, whom she presented as a great psychological novelist displaying great depth, truth, wholeness in his portraits of people (*Bleter*, III, 211). So Cahan kept in touch with literary values, which he was beginning to discern more fully in himself as he wrote his stories and articles for the *Arbeiter Tseitung*. In 1888 he read *Anna Karenina* again, found it more interesting, but literature was still largely a side interest with him.

It wasn't until he had been in America almost ten years that he felt he could truly appreciate Tolstoy. Interestingly enough, the catalytic experience was a reading of Chekhov. A friend to whom he'd shown his first story gave him a copy of Chekhov's *Crimean People* to read. The book revolutionized Cahan's conception of fiction. At first he could not believe that such simple scenes could be something to write about, yet Chekhov took him unerringly to the heart of life. After that he read *Anna Karenina* for the third time, and he saw how deeply and closely Tolstoy had penetrated to the spirit of his people. In America,

Cahan realized, he had grown, learned, knew "an ocean of types
of people." He had learned himself to look closely at life—so
now he could at last appreciate Tolstoy. A new literary self was
being born in the editor of the *Arbeiter Tseitung* (*Bleter,* IV,
17–18).

On one of his trips to Europe as a delegate to the Socialist International Congresses, Cahan arranged to see his parents for the
first time since he had left home. Only about a decade had
passed, but his visit with them emphasized the great gulf between him and his parents in almost every respect imaginable,
and between his earlier life and his present one. His experience,
of course, was only a heightened and dramatic version of something familiar to thousands. Trying to understand change, putting
together the fragmentation resulting from geographic, historical,
spiritual dislocation experienced by living people was to become
Cahan's great subject. It was all around him and it was in him.
One could deal with these realities discursively and theoretically,
write or translate grand historical and sociological syntheses
that explained it all—but to put it together in the realm of feeling, art, and imagination, as Chekhov and Tolstoy had shown,
could not only honorably serve, but might provide the only real
"thrill of truth."

CHAPTER THREE

Stories and Language on the Road to *Yekl*

Yiddish Stories

Cahan began to write fiction cautiously—that is, in Yiddish, in the pages of the *Arbeiter Tseitung,* where critical tastes in literature were as yet largely unformed. Nevertheless, his first story, "Mottke Arbel and His Romance" (1892), was a more than respectable performance, embodying a new literary voice and sensibility. The story tells of a low-bred fellow whose modest business success in America enables him to contract to marry the daughter of his former employer and social superior in Russia, but who is frustrated in the end because the young woman becomes engaged to another man on the journey to America. Even this cursory summary shows the undercutting of "romance" suggested in the title; "Mottke Arbel" displays a sure sense of the Jewish immigrant experience and a lively feeling for real character, dialogue, situation. It was a great success with Cahan's readers.

Cahan's first English story was a translation and version of this one. As "A Providential Match," (1895) the story was to have fateful consequences for Cahan's career when it attracted the attention of William Dean Howells. On the basis of that story Howells urged Cahan to attempt a longer work on the experiences of the ghetto—the genesis of *Yekl.* But more of that (and a full discussion of "A Providential Match") later.

Encouraged by the reception of his first story, Cahan undertook a longer work in Yiddish, which went on for many issues in the *Arbeiter Tseitung* in 1894, and which had an even greater impact on his readers than the earlier effort. Called "Rafael Naarizokh iz Gevoren a Sozialist" ("Rafael Naarizokh Becomes a Socialist")—and subtitled in its book version "The Story of a Carpenter Who Came to His Senses"—it was a didactic tale about a simple immigrant's awakening class-consciousness in America and his conversion to socialism.[1] Largely a vehicle for transmitting socialist ideas to the readers of the journal, the story avoids aridity by its concrete details of street, shop and café and its overall wit and good humor. The real strength of the story as it drags on (occasionally) through many episodes and twenty-one chapters is the sympathetically conceived and presented character of the naive Rafael.

A carpenter in his native village of Kriletz, Rafael Radetsky is extremely honest, speaks his mind, hates lies—and so is thought something of a fool. He is a gifted artisan who likes good work, a good bean stew, the singing of a good cantor. His nickname "Naarizokh" comes from the name of a portion of the sabbath service that he continually hums and sings while engrossed in his work. Above all, although without education, Rafael likes to think and reflect on just about everything. A letter from his brother in America describing glowing conditions (he could make $10 a week as a carpenter in America, besides there being no Czar and tax assessor) induces him and his wife Sara Gitl to emigrate. They sell all that they own for $45 and go to New York.

He soon discovers that the New World is no golden land. Almost immediately he learns that the many "machines"—a word that in Kriletz referred only to locomotives—employed in America's shops meant amazing productivity, but not, to his surprise, more rewards for those who worked the machines. As a countryman tells him, he is truly a "greenhorn" to possess such a simple idea. Factory work and mass-production techniques are entirely new and alienating to Rafael. In his first job he is whacked on the back by the foreman and told to shut up ("Sharrup!") or be fired when he starts singing his familiar "naarizokh." He stops singing, feels defeated and shamed, no longer the man he was formerly; his wife, too, is lonely and forlorn as she sits in her dreary East Side apartment—both regret leaving Kriletz.

Within six months, Rafael has aged ten years. But in his thoughts he has also lived ten years. He reflects continually on his situation—a boss who is more concerned with his machine (which Rafael is expected to attend like a robot) than with him, the disparity between East Side ghetto streets and Fifth Avenue, the existence of rich and poor. At first he blames the machines for all his and other workers' troubles, but in an argument with his wife he talks himself into a new idea: machines themselves are not the cause of misfortune—in fact, they ease his work—but rather it is the ownership of them that is the root problem. He pursues this insight with great excitement—if only he owned the machines . . . but one man alone cannot run a factory . . . so if many workers got together and bought a factory they could then be the bosses and live well! But where to get the money?

As he continues to work in different furniture factories these ideas are further refined and he gains new insights into the system. He learns that bosses are not necessarily enviable—they are caught in a savagely competitive situation and can be ruined at any time: the big fish eat the little fish. When he learns about monopolies and their control of prices, he concludes that a single cooperatively run factory could not succeed. He arrives at the notion that a super-machine, above all the others, that would make them all work rationally is really needed. This he calls his "song of songs," which would make the workers rejoice. The more he thinks about the world, the more it seems a prison to him and that he needs a plan of escape to a wider, more beautiful world.

In a conversation about the new technology, he realizes that the achievement of such a plan is not impossible: surely a "song of songs" should not be more difficult to invent than the telephone, telegraph or horseless carriage! One day, short two cents for his fare on an elevated train, he walks across the bridge from

Brooklyn to New York. Once there had been a charge for this walk, but it had been dropped as soon as the cost of building the bridge was repaid. The bridge now belongs to the community, the train to a private owner. Suddenly all becomes clear to Rafael. The answer is community-owned trains—and then why not community-owned bread and clothing factories? In the idea of public ownership of *everything* he has discovered his "song of songs."

Immensely excited, Rafael wants to bring this idea to the whole world, which he feels sure will accept it and put it into effect at once. What he needs, he believes in his innocence, is to take out a patent on the idea. He gets a lawyer, who quickly sizes him up as a "damn fool" and obligingly agrees to get him a patent in three days for twenty-five dollars. The days and the fees stretch on, but of course Rafael receives no patent, and is ultimately thrown out by the lawyer.

Still bemused by his dream, Rafael responds to a leaflet that announces a meeting promising to explain why the workers are miserable, and what they can do to make their existence a paradise. In great anticipation he attends the meeting and discovers, much to his surprise, that his "song of songs" has a name—Socialism— and that he is, in fact, a Socialist. This knowledge comes in a strange new language, in many long speeches, frequently too abstract for his simple concrete turn of mind (when Rafael decides to speak his full mind from the floor it causes much good-natured laughter at the meeting). But it does come, and he soon becomes a passionate convert to Socialism. The goals of liberty, equality and fraternity which the Socialists claim as their own enrapture him and the "Marseillaise," he himself reflects, replaces the "Naarizokh."

His transformation is completed through a relationship with a café intellectual and socialist named Vicker. From him Rafael learns about Science and Nature (which brings him out of the darkness of his religious superstitions), dialectics (as difficult to him, and as intellectually tempting, as Gemorrah), political and economic class-war, the history of social organization, and, finally, the need to remove from love and marriage any trace of economic interest. In becoming a socialist, Rafael has become

a new man—he has shaved his beard (with mixed feelings), taken
pains with his wardrobe and personal hygiene, looks and acts
younger (as does his wife, prodded by his example), is capable
of abstract discourse—in short, he has become, as one of the
chapter headings affirms, "Not richer, not more pious, but more
of a *mentsch* [more of a person]."

As can be seen from this summary, there are long stretches
of theorizing in *Rafael Naarizokh*—several chapters are devoted
to the speeches at the crucial meeting attended by Rafael, others
to Vicker's patient exposition of the socialist line on everything. Yet the book does not quite sink under this weight, or
survive merely as an extended pamphlet. Action and development are minimal, to be sure, in any traditional fictional sense—
—it is episodic, and the characteristic "action" is a speech, conversation, or inner reflection on a social idea. But as all of it
serves to illuminate the straightforwardness and wonder of Rafael's consciousness, it can be read sympathetically. The vernac-
ular, too, works to take the curse off arid theory—in Rafael's
homey translations of abstruse matters, in Sara Gitl's crusty
responses to his efforts to enlighten her, in the American-English learned and needed by the characters (a glossary of 145
such terms is appended to the volume: among them "barber,"
"boss," "furniture," "party," "wages"). All in all, *Rafael
Naarizokh* displays the developed skill of Cahan as the old Proletarian Maggid and Hester Street Reporter, who can take a
small concrete incident or insight—no charge for walking across
a bridge, let us say—and develop it into a larger general idea.
The overall achievement of this book lies in its coherence, de-
riving from the socialist spirit informing it, and the charm of its
central character.

Cahan published one other story in the *Arbeiter Tseitung*—
"Di Tswei Shidokhim" ("The Two Matches")—which he later
thought the best short story in either language he wrote in his
early period.

The story concerns Harris and his friend Jake and their marriages [to Becky and her aunt]. Harris is an installment agent,
lively and good looking, who woos Becky too ardently. She allows him to kiss her, but then regrets it, thinking he may

consider her "cheap." Although she likes Harris, she refuses to marry him. She almost immediately regrets *that* decision, but it is too late to rectify it. A few weeks afterwards, Harris marries Mrs. Zager, Becky's widowed aunt. Jake meanwhile consoles Becky. He is aroused by her, and though Jake seems less attractive than Harris, Becky marries him. At the story's end, both marriages have foundered—Jake abandons Becky after a few months; Harris is revealed to be a lazy and worthless charmer.

Slight as the tale may seem, the situation and characters are unforced and credible, and Cahan reveals a fine sensitivity towards psychological states of mind and the subtlety, new in his work, of awakening sexuality. This element in the work may account for Cahan's decision not to convert the story into English for an American audience. In matters of social theory and sex he seems less restrained with his Jewish audience. On the other hand, he published the story under one of his two *Arbeiter Tseitung* pseudonyms, Sotzius (the other, David Bernstein, was used for his Tolstoy translation), which indicates an attitude not without ambiguity towards them or towards his emerging identity as a writer. It was the last story he wrote in the Yiddish language for several years.

English Stories

Cahan's first stories in English, "A Providential Match," and "A Sweatshop Romance," were included in *The Imported Bridegroom,* a collection of five stories published in 1898,[2] two years after the success of *Yekl.* But they appeared first in the magazine *Short Story* in 1895, so it will be useful to focus upon them at this point as forerunners of the more significant *Yekl.*

They may both be considered somewhat slight stories, but "A Providential Match" shows real talent, and even the less interesting and successful one, "A Sweatshop Romance," flashes to life occasionally as it depicts a locale new to American fiction, the tenement sweat-shop. Cahan later preferred "Di Tswei Shidokhim" because he thought the people in that story, their speech, relationships, spirit, were (despite a bad ending), more

natural and full of life than the others; but this kind of judgment only points to the difficulty of Cahan's often ambiguous
relation to the languages he worked in.

The original Yiddish title of "A Providential Match," it will
be remembered, was "Mottke Arbel and His Romance." To the
Yiddish audience, the title reveals the coarse, somewhat comic
nature of the story's central character. Mottke is a familiar di-
minutive that can be slightly patronizing, while "Arbel" is Yiddish for "sleeve." In the opening paragraph of the English
version, the narrator explains the significance of the hero's curious nickname, "Rouvke Arbel"(his American name is Robert
Friedman): "Before he came to America, and when he still
drove horses and did all sorts of work for Peretz the distiller, he
was in the habit of assigning to the sleeves of his sheepskin coat
such duties as generally devolve upon a pocket handkerchief."
(122). Cahan changed the name Mottke to Rouvke, the dimin-
utive of Rouven, because it seemed more understandable to the
audience in English. That audience might lose the significance
of his former occupation, as well—the word for a drayman in
Yiddish ("balegolah") is the word for a coarse, low-bred type
of person. After four years in America, the narrator tells us,
Rouven is "now quite a different young man in a different coat
and with a handkerchief in its side-pocket." He is also the proud
possessor of a business card in English ("his diploma"): "Robert
Friedman, Dealer in Furniture, Carpets, Jewelry, Clothing, Ladies Dress Goods, etc. Weekly Payments Taken." He took the
name Robert instead of Reuben because he thought it had a
more "tzibilized" sound to it. (126)

The basic elements of many Cahan stories can already be discerned: the superior narrator explaining to a reader, whose values he presumably shares, some inside information about the
Jewish immigrant culture in America. The emphasis will be on
the effects of the culture-clash upon the immigrant. In this case,
the protagonist is faintly comic, although a success (on some
level) in busines, and "Americanized" in his name, dress, and on
the crudest level of deportment. He is a "freed man" in America, but as the story shows, he is not fully liberated. Much of his

old character and ethos remain, while his grasp of the new ethos is partial, crude, superficial. New coat and business card notwithstanding, the laugh finally *is* on him.

The story is as follows: Rouvke has done relatively well in America, but despite his efforts at self-improvement and meeting "yoong laddas," he is still a bachelor. Reb Feive, a *shadchen* (marriage broker) enters the picture. He convinces Rouvke that he can negotiate a match with Hanele, the previously inaccessible daughter of Peretz, Rouvke's former employer and the first citizen of Kropovetz in Russia. Rouvke always felt great tenderness for the lovely Hanele, but such a match would have been unthinkable in the old village. He wondered, too, if he wouldn't be better off in a business way to marry a merchant's daughter who could bring him a dowry. Feive prevails, however, and letters sail back and forth between New York and Kropovetz. At first Peretz is outraged at the suggestion that his former *balegolah* aspires to wed his refined and accomplished daughter. Gradually, however, Peretz comes to reflect that she is in her twenty-fifth year and no new suitors had recently appeared, and that America did indeed make new men. The glowing account of the *shadchen* about Rouvke's piety, success, education and general excellence (all wild exaggerations) take effect and Peretz consents to the match. Hanele, being a "true daughter of Israel," soon acquiesces in her father's decision. Rouvke is delighted and sends enough money (to Rouvke the "only fly in the ointment") for her clothes and transportation. When the time comes for her to arrive, Rouvke waits excitedly at Castle Garden with carriages and in the company of friends. Hanele arrives, charming and beautiful, but on the arm of a young man in the seedy uniform of a Russian collegian. She and this man, called Levinsky (how curious that this name appears in Cahan's first and last fiction—probably an echo of Levin from *Anna Karenina,* the work that meant so much to Cahan), had met on shipboard, where the moon was the best *shadchen*—they had fallen in love, in a true "Providential Match." Rouvke is stunned, but cannot do anything except exclaim, in Yiddish, "I want my hundred and fifty dollars back!," and then in English, "I call a politzman. I vant my hoonred an' fifty dollar." Rouvke is brushed aside by a burly employee of an immigrant hotel who takes Hanele and Levinsky away. Rouvke is speechless, Reb Feive wrings his hands, and the young peddlers Rouvke had brought along to show his triumph now bandy "whispered jokes."

Despite its apparent simplicity, and the O. Henry quality of the ending, Cahan gets a good deal into his story. He tells the American reader many things about Jewish life and customs, about the new immigrant's experience in America, and Rouvke's climb in business. But what marks the story off is Cahan's sensitivity to character and theme. He presents a careful analysis of motive and behavior in Rouvke and Peretz, shrewdly showing the interplay of each as they realistically appraise their situations. An earthy material incentive is shown to combine with the longing in their hearts about Hanele. The laugh is certainly on Rouvke at the end, but it is somewhat chilling. That Rouvke is left speechless is a fine touch. There is a real sense of loss, but he is incapable of expressing precisely the nature of his loss. Shylock had cried "My ducats! My daughter!" when he lost Jessica, placing money before the human relationship. That seems to be Rouvke's first, almost instinctual cry ("My hundred and fifty dollars!"), but that is clearly a displacement, not the real or central loss he feels. There is a poignant note in his inability, in a new language and in a hostile environment (the burly runner who pushes him aside, his unsympathetic colleagues), to express his innermost feelings. Cahan strikes this note—a theme of longing, unfulfillment, and essential loneliness—early, continues it through many stories in various guises, until its culmination in the complicated and final statement of *The Rise of David Levinsky*.

In a story like "A Providential Match" we are aware of several verbal structures, languages, operating simultaneously. There is the immigrant's English—crude, to a native speaker often comic; there is the language of low-life America, both directly and indirectly coming through in the immigrant—in other stories there may be other, more ordinary or even refined American speech; there is Yiddish in translation by the narrator, usually as simple as the characters, but nevertheless more supple and resonant than any ostentatiously sophisticated English, which tends to be lifeless, although acceptable to the best literary taste of the time. This pattern, with variations, of course, will appear in most of Cahan's work.

Upon the success of "A Providential Match," Cahan quickly wrote "A Sweat-Shop Romance." This is less complicated in almost every respect than the first story, but not without some characteristic and interesting touches.

The sweat shop of the title is the three-room tenement apartment of Leizer Lipman, a "contract tailor." Besides Leizer and his wife Zlate, there are four workers in the shop: Meyer the presser, Heyman the operator, Beile the finisher, David the baster. Beile and Heyman are interested in each other, although Heyman is too timid to propose to her. All the relationships are transformed suddenly when Zlate, trying to impress some visitors, tries to treat Beile like a domestic, ordering her to go out to buy some soda pop. David, the shop joker, urges Beile to refuse to go. Zlate is angered; Beile and David quit their jobs. Heyman had sat silently throughout the altercation, too intimidated to speak out. For two weeks following the incident, Heyman cannot screw up the courage necessary to visit Beile and commiserate with her. When he finally does go to her apartment, he is in time to overhear the conclusion of David and Beile's wedding ceremony.

The story is obviously slight—the ending especially caused Cahan distress when he later reflected on it ("how on earth did it pop into my head?"), although he explained it away on the grounds that it was the sort of thing American audiences at the time expected. With all its faults and inconsequentiality, the story does provide a good picture of a shop, the crowding, the scramble for work when the boss entered with his "bundles"; more than anything else there is the retained and recognizable humanity of the people, however crudely presented or however crudely they presented themselves (Zlate is a bit of a ranting hysteric, not a person). The portrayal of the sweat-shop was not as stark as Jacob Riis's account, but Cahan was making an effort to show his characters as rounded people, not merely victims of a system. He erred in ending his small tale in a romantic glow, although even in this regard, because his characters did not really possess the vocabulary of love (it was something Beile had only *heard* of), there is authenticity in the flat-footed exposition and dialogue. This story should be seen as essentially transitional and experimental. *Yekl* would provide a greater challenge and achievement.

Which Language?

Cahan was restlessly moving between various worlds during the years of his earliest literary ventures, and to some extent this uneasiness shows in them, although not necessarily in obvious and literal ways. In addition to his immense activity in these years as editor, translator, journalist, he made three trips to Europe as a socialist delegate to international congresses. On his last trip in 1894 he went as a companion to an American friend, James K. Paulding, who was eager to have Cahan's running commentary and impressions of the scenes, events, personalities they encountered. This role may have kindled in Cahan a perception of his great potential as an interpreter to the broader English-reading public of the materials of his radical, Russian-Jewish world. The medium of this interpretation, obviously, would have to be the English language.

Despite the success of *Rafael Naarizokh,* or his own high regard for "Di Tswei Shidokhim," a literary career in the conditions of the 1890s meant for Cahan writing in English. The prevailing attitude among Jewish intellectuals and much of the middle-class towards Yiddish was that it was a sub-literary jargon, incapable of a rich and subtle literature. As we have seen, this was a view that Cahan certainly did not wholly share. He was sympathetic to the substantial development of the Yiddish stage, and was aware of and appreciated the birth of serious Yiddish literature then taking place. In the year he re-read *Anna Karenina* for the third time he also published and wrote enthusiastically about the first stories to appear in America by the great Yiddish writer I.L. Peretz, and in the year of *Yekl* he was writing appreciatively and shrewdly about Sholem Aleichem. Nevertheless, the Yiddish audience in America was small and relatively unsophisticated, and the term "Yiddish Literature" was then something of a joke (*Bleter*, IV, 20).

In his memoirs Cahan tells of an experience that crystallized for him his feelings about the language he would have to write in if he was to have a serious literary career. At the Zurich Socialist Congress he encountered several sympathetic Bulgarian and Rumanian delegates, Jews and writers. Their situation seemed to parallel and illuminate his own. These writers knew they were cut off from readers outside their native countries (few of whom could be expected to learn Bulgarian or Rumanian), so that if they wanted to reach a significant audience that would take their work seriously, they would have to write in one of the great languages of the world. Cahan believed that his situation as a Yiddish writer in America was analogous to theirs.

The question came down to one of an audience, therefore, and the inevitable writer's problem of relationship to that audience. For Cahan, socialist, Jew, Realist, immigrant, the problem of the right balance to be struck with a potential American reading public was an acute one.

Cahan was uniquely qualified to render the subject of his fiction, although he did not always resolve satisfactorily the complicated pull of subject, audience, and his complex vision. He had sympathy for the Jews, his people, but as a Realist he eschewed mere advocacy and tendentiousness. He understood the limitation of the Jewish immigrant—indeed one of his self-proclaimed tasks for more than a dozen years had been to help bring a semi-literate, largely uneducated and backward people (despite the high value placed on learning in the Jewish ethos, this was the truth about most of them) into the contemporary and enlightened world. On the other hand, a feeling of gross superiority would be offensive and, indeed, un-socialist, although there was always an elitist element in his socialism. He felt, too, the old ideal of speaking to and identifying with a larger humanity, although he never felt the need to emancipate himself entirely from a Jewish past. Modulating all these tensions was the pity and compassion for the human condition that he absorbed from the Russian writers. As we have seen, Cahan asked for truth in dealing with Jewish life, despising "shund" literature (slapstick caricature) or its counterpart in inflated rhetoric and historical melodrama. He knew the "greenhorn" and what was happening to him was an important subject and that it should be presented without ridicule or romance. It cannot be said that Cahan always achieved equilibrium amidst the contending forces; the balance was always perilous. That he achieved it at all, as I think he does in *Yekl* and with far more complex material in *Levinsky,* is remarkable.

For obvious reasons, Cahan was fascinated by the differences among languages as well as the class and character differentiations within a language. For him, Russian was the embodiment of his intellectual life, Yiddish of the emotional, English of the fascinating and rich "other" world, the mastery of which was a measure of one's sophistication and status. Language, of course, is the embodiment of culture, and everywhere in Cahan's work we see his attention to linguistic expressions of the clashes between and within cultures.

CHAPTER FOUR

Cultural Interaction: *Yekl* and Howells

Yekl: A Tale of the New York Ghetto (1896)[1] is a book that
should be better known; now that the successful film *Hester
Street* has been based on it, perhaps it will be. No one today
would claim that it is a neglected masterpiece of American literature—as could be said until recently about Kate Chopin's *The
Awakening* (1899)—but it deals vividly with issues still very
much alive in pluralistic America. The problematic effect of a
dominant culture upon people of various cultural legacies—in
the case of *Yekl* upon a Jewish immigrant, Jake Podgorny—is
a condition of national life still very much with us.

Cahan's Jake is not a very appealing character as he succumbs
to the superficial and only partially understood aspects of the
larger culture, a fact that angered some of Cahan's Jewish readers, who thought he could have found more admirable types to
write about in English. Leaving aside for the moment this vex-
ing question, it must be noted that his story opened up territory
new to American consciousness. *Yekl* is the first novel, so far as
I know, *by* an immigrant wholly about the immigrant experience. As much as the story itself, its genesis and reception—in
which the dean of American letters, William Dean Howells,
played a crucial role—suggests what is at stake in Cahan's pioneering effort. Close attention to the assumptions and ambigu-

ities in Cahan's tale, in Howells' relation to it, and in the relation of the two men to each other—the burden of this chapter—
will yield valuable insights, I believe, into an enduring problem
of American culture generally. Let us turn first to the tale itself.

The Story of Yekl

It is a short book, more a long story than a novel, about a callow immigrant's adaptation to the mores of the new land. The
essential elements of the story, which is divided into ten chapters, can be quickly summarized: After only three years in
America, Jake Podgorny discards almost all his old world values
while acquiring a crude smattering of the new. He repudiates
and finally divorces the wife he had at first left behind, then
takes a more "Americanized" one. He has experimented with an
emotion called "love," and feels stirring in himself, however
partially and barely articulated, feelings of guilt and uncertainty
about his condition. Thus the barest résumé of the book. An
appreciation of the full import of the material requires a more
detailed chapter-by-chapter account, as follows.

In the first chapter, entitled "Jake and Yekl," we are informed that Jake's old world name had been "Yekl," and we
see him at work in a New York cloak factory. He shows off his
English and knowledge of American sports to his shopmates,
rattling off some names of celebrities: "John Shullivan," "Chol-
ly Meetchel." He prides himself on being Americanized; in only
three years he seems to have cast off his old identity: "Once I
live in America, I want to know that I live in America. *Dot'sh
a kin a man I am!* [this expression becomes his tagline throughout the book] One must not be a *greenhorn*." (Cahan informs
the reader in a footnote that "English words incorporated in the
Yiddish of the characters of this narrative are given in italics.")
Taunted by some shopmates for putting on the airs of a Yankee
and for being rather crude, Jake becomes gloomy and reflects
upon his past. We learn that he had left home for economic reasons—his father's smithy could not support two families— and
that, unbeknownst to his fellow workers or the girls he takes to

a local dancing academy, there are a wife and child at home in the old village, waiting to be sent for.

In the second chapter, "The New York Ghetto," despite his new determination to bring his wife and child over and begin a new life, and to stay away from Joe Peltner's dancing academy, Jake gravitates towards the dance hall. He is soon caught up in its hectic activity, where he is the cock of the walk. When he leaves the hall it is with Fanny the Preacher (who works in the same shop as Jake) on one arm and blond Mamie Fein on the other—his resolution to send for his wife now in the indefinite future. In the third chapter, "In the Grip of His Past," however, he learns in a letter from home that his father has died. (Jake is illiterate, so the letter is read to him by one of the professional "readers" in the ghetto who makes a precarious living in this way.) Overcome with guilt and nostalgia, he determines anew to send for Gitl and his son Yossele. This time he obeys his good impulse and they do arrive, in the fourth chapter, "The Meeting."

Yekl is dismayed at the utterly old-world and, to his Americanized eyes, dowdy appearance of Gitl, in her shapeless garment and the bulky wig worn by Orthodox married women. She in turn is overwhelmed by her husband's shaven face and smart clothes, which make him look as a nobleman would at home, and by his casual disregard of the Jewish Sabbath laws. Nevertheless, in the next chapter, "A Paterfamilias," both seem determined to make some adjustments so that the marriage will work out. Gitl consents to being called "Goitie" (Gertie) although it is close enough to the Yiddish word for Gentile to make her uneasy. Under the prodding of an officious neighbor, Mrs. Kavarsky, she will now wear a corset in a vain attempt to give shape to her home-sewn dress, and she entertains the thought of giving up her wig and kerchief. For Gitl, the two images—her Yekl and the American Jake—are beginning to merge into a single person. Jake, on his part, can work himself up to a proper feeling of dignity, in his good moments, at the thought of his pure and faithful wife (so much better, he thinks, than the loose women at the dancing academy) and his attractive son. Just as things look as if they might work out, Mamie Fein pays them an unexpected visit.

Talking mostly in English, Mamie demands payment of twenty-five dollars which Yekl had borrowed from her, presumably for his wife's passage money. It is obvious that Mamie is smarting with jealous anger. She presents a fine appearance and talks with Jake mostly in English, so Gitl suspects that they are not, as Jake says, talking "business"—for when he does that with their boarder Bernstein (also a fellow-worker of Jake's) they always talk in Yiddish. In "Circumstances Alter Cases," the sixth chapter, Gitl consults Mrs. Kavarsky, who gives her the same advice about improving her appearance in order to hold her husband; moreover, Mrs. Kavarsky suggests going to the law should Jake abandon her. Gitl is more distressed than ever.

Meanwhile Jake finds Mamie's image haunting him. He seeks her out in her room, asks her to come out for a talk in the street. They quarrel and he leaves in an unsatisfied frame of mind; her image more than ever unsettles him and he begins to think he is in love with her—a strange, new idea. Jake's meeting with Mamie on Essex Street had been witnessed by a friend of Fanny the Preacher, who had quit the shop when she discovered Jake was married. Fanny comes now to Gitl to tell her that Mamie has set her cap for Jake and wants to take him away from her. Panicked and grief-stricken, Gitl repairs again to Mrs. Kavarsky (chapter seven, "Mrs. Kavarsky's Coup D'Etat") who loquaciously, righteously, and obtusely is still convinced that it will all come out right if she modernizes Gitl's hair style. She does just that, presents her to Jake—and he is revolted. In the ensuing discussion, Mrs. Kavarsky and Jake quarrel bitterly, a quarrel fed by his anxiety and guilt at being seen with "dantzing-hall" girls. Jake storms out of the apartment, fantasying an escape to some other place, perhaps even to London.

He rushes to Mamie's lodging, hoping she will have money enough for his passage, or, if necessary, for both of them. In "A Housetop Idyll," (chapter eight), Jake and Mamie declare their love for each other and make plans for his divorce—after she receives guarantees of his truthfulness. Jake will go to Philadelphia to stay with a relative of hers while divorce proceedings will be undertaken at Mamie's expense. Afterwards they will marry.

The penultimate chapter, "The Parting," depicts the final stage of the divorce several months later. In the last chapter, "A Defeated Victor," Gitl appears considerably smartened up, her appearance Americanized. She is at first doleful, but brightens as she contemplates the grocery business she and Bernstein—she and her former boarder have wed—will start with the money (Mamie's) settled upon her by Jake. Jake and Mamie meanwhile are on a trolley car bound for city hall, where they are to be married. His feelings are mixed: a burden is removed, but a dark and impenetrable future looms ahead. Instead of being a victor, he feels he has been the victim of an ignominious defeat. As the tale ends he is reluctant to have the car reach its destination.

As usual, Cahan gets a great deal of local color into his story; the scenes in the shop as the people set to work on their machines, the swarming streets of the East Side, the uproarious dancing academy, illuminate an important social reality. Cahan is not averse to stopping the action for the sake of a two-page didactic essay on the ghetto and its occupants, of which the following is an excerpt:

> Suffolk Street is in the very thick of the battle for breath. For it lies in the heart of that part of the East Side which has within the last two or three decades become the Ghetto of the American metropolis, and, indeed, the metropolis of the Ghettos of the world. It is one of the most densely populated spots on the face of the earth—a seething human sea fed by streams, streamlets, and rills of immigration flowing from all the Yiddish-speaking centres of Europe. Hardly a block but shelters Jews from every nook and corner of Russia, Poland, Galicia, Hungary, Roumania; Lithuanian Jews, Bessarabian Jews. . . . people with all sorts of antecedents, tastes, habits, inclinations, and speaking all sorts of subdialects of the same jargon, thrown pellmell into one social caldron—a human hodge-podge with its component parts changed but not yet fused into one homogeneous whole. (28–30)

Such an explanatory essay, much like many of his newspaper *feuilletons*, is aimed at explaining to the American reader a social phenomenon that might, at first, seem threatening or merely exotic and bizarre. A resident of the Ghetto might resent being considered part of "a hodgepodge," yet Cahan performs here an important task for the Jewish population as well. He acknowledges the uniqueness of Jewish experience, but shows that it is perfectly comprehensible, not ineffably alien, above all rich and full. A few years later he will perform the same function as mediator and interpreter for Hutchins Hapgood, acting as his guide on the East Side while Hapgood will gather the materials and impressions that became *The Spirit of the Ghetto,* a classic American book that is abundant in its sympathy, respect, admiration for the Jewish immigrant culture.

Cahan fills in much about Jewish customs: Jake's recall of Sabbath procedure in the old *shtetl* (village), the behavior proper to Orthodox wives, the details and manner of an Orthodox Jewish divorce. Behind the characters there is always the reflection of shtetl values and an ethos that would have permeated the behavior of Jews in the old country, and whose absence in Jake emphasizes his vulgarity. Jake displays much defensive-aggressiveness at having his *prost* (common, ignorant) qualities recalled by his more literate shopmates, who don't believe that his proudly displayed American interests—sport and dancing— are especially significant human activities. They value learning and self-improvement. Jake quickly realizes that New York Jews, living in self-contained neighborhoods, retain more of the older values than the Boston Jews he had worked with when he first came to America and from whom he acquired his strong drive towards acculturation.

The potential weakness of all local color writing is that meticulous recording of the material can become an end in itself. Cahan avoids this potential limitation, I believe, by an adroit balancing act. One cannot say the material and local color is always subordinated to character and theme—at its best, however, the novel holds these elements in an artful equilibrium. The colorful material is played out upon a credible and interesting narrative and the characters often leap surprisingly to life.

The major figures are not one-sided in their presentation. That
there are doubts, fears, shifts and changes in the consciousness
of Mamie, Gitl, even Jake, is evident. And a major theme, that
of dislocation and acculturation, winds sinuously throughout
the story, presenting now comic, now tragic, potentialities to
the discerning reader.

This theme is served most graphically in the language of the
tale. The point-of-view of the narrator is superior but equivocal
in relation to both his audience and the story itself. He lectures
the American audience—recall the lengthy quotation on the
genesis of New York's East Side Ghetto—presumably as an
equal, sharing information, but with sympathy and some pride
in the people, dispelling, really, an implicit prejudice and ignorance in his audience. Regrettably he is capable also of an arch
and condescending attitude towards his Jewish characters. Their
fractured English is comic when it is not grotesque:

> "Jimmie Corbett *leaked* him, and Jimmie *leaked* Cholly
> Meetchel, too ... *You can betch you' bootsh!* ... But Jim-
> mie *pundished* him. *Oh, didn't he knock him out of shight!*
> ... He *tzettled* him in three *roynds.* ..."
> "What is a *rawned*, Djake," the presser asked. (4)

Or it is crude and vulgar, adopting the worst parts of the dominant culture:

> "Don' shpeak English. She'll t'ink I don' knu vot ve
> shpeakin' "
> "Vot d'I care vot she t'inks? She's your vife, ain' it? Vell,
> she mus' know ev'ryt'ing. Dot's right! A husban' dass'n't
> hide not'ink from his vife! ...
> "Shurr-r up, Mamie!". ...
> "Don't'ch you like it, lump it!" (107)

"This dialogue is as painful to read as Henry Roth's in *Call It
Sleep,* where the ugliness of the new, ill-mastered language is
contrasted with the more humane language of their inner selves,
and it is as cruel as anything by Arthur Kober.

Cahan mercilessly shows Jake's callowness as a creature incapable of deep reflection—as when he decides impulsively to

rush from his family to Mamie's apartment after his quarrel
with Mrs. Kavarsky. If Cahan reveals hints of greater depths in
Jake and others, they are invariably cultural carry-overs from
the *shtetl* past, as when Jake feels such sorrow at his father's
death that he prays for him and resolves to live a more righteous
life. The burden of the tale reveals, however, that the new American experience cuts this better part away, leaving Jake (and
Mamie) naked to their partially understood and only half-artic-
ulated desires and fantasies.

Their love scene on the housetop is central, containing all
the elements mentioned above. The scene is framed in a semi-
comic mode: the laundry hanging on the lines there on the roof
takes on a ghostly, quasi-symbolic form in Jake's fevered imagination. During the colloquy with Mamie he thinks of them as
graveyard shrouds, which remind him of his past. "While she
was speaking, his attention had been attracted to a loosened pillowcase ominously fluttering and flopping a yard or two off.
The figure of his dead father, attired in burial linen, uprose to
his mind" (164). As Jake is taking the step into unchartered
emotional waters—divorce, but chiefly into an affair of passion,
love, so foreign to the old values—the pillowcase flaps loudly,
"sternly, warningly, portentously" (165). The whole scene
would collapse into bathos, but there is real emotion struggling
for expression. "I cannot tell it so well," he says, pointing to
his heart (161). "Love" in the western sense was foreign to the
shtetl ethos, and Jake had been in the United States only three
years, after all. Cahan's achievement is to show that the new,
imperfectly assimilated language (and the values they represented) could not in the mouths and hearts of these immigrants
achieve mature felicity. Their struggle for it would be alternately
comic, vulgar, or touching. It remained for later generations, the
descendants of these immigrants, to master the new language
and culture and in its own terms present a fuller expression of
human possibility.

Above all, Cahan was aware of the transforming, almost mag-
ical quality of the American experience upon these people. Ignorant and callow as he is, Yekl is nevertheless able to reflect
as follows:

During the three years since he had set foot on the soil, where a "shister (Yiddish for shoemaker) becomes a mister and a mister a shister," he had lived so much more than three years—so much more, in fact, than in all the twenty-two years of his previous life—that his Russian past appeared to him a dream and his wife and child, together with his former self, fellow-characters in a charming tale, which he was neither willing to banish from his memory nor able to reconcile with the actualities of his American present. (53–54)

The American experience was strange, thrilling, exhilirating—the sense of life and its possibilities heightened in its ambiance as nowhere else—but clashing with a dreamlike past that exerts its force and demands to be reconciled with the new reality. In the absence of such a reconciliation, personality remains fractured, incomplete. The theme haunts Cahan's fiction. In *Yekl* the seriousness of this theme threatens to be lost whenever Jake resembles a caricature—his comic versions of the English language seem fare for the vaudeville stage—but the irony and knowingness of the superior authorial voice ensure a broader reading of what is, finally, a significant cautionary tale.

Howells and Cahan: Hailing "A New Star of Realism"

The full significance of *Yekl* cannot be considered apart from Howells' role in its inception, publication and reception. In his sponsorship of the work Howells helped to broaden and enrich the country's literary heritage, in the face of a prevailing parochialism of taste. On the other hand, the terms of his acceptance and support of the book reveal some of his own middle-class limits as a critic. Howells stood, in a sense, at the very center of high culture in America—what that meant and how it conditioned his response to Cahan's work can be seen, I believe, as an important moment in our cultural history. The Howells-Cahan relationship flowered briefly, but it was important. It led to a work that broke new ground in American literature and to Cahan's being taken seriously as a literary figure—it sheds light, as well, upon certain persistent problems of culture and its control.[2]

Howells first met Cahan in 1892, when he was doing research for the opening sections of *A Traveler From Altruria,* in which he needed to know at first hand something about "walking delegates" (union organizers). He heard about the editor of the socialist *Arbeiter Tseitung* and went to a café on the East Side to find him. Cahan wasn't there, but Howells left his card, asking Cahan to come to see him. Cahan was flattered by this attention from the dean of American literature, and went to see Howells at his home. Howells was surprised by Cahan, who certainly did not conform to the stereotype of a union organizer. Much to Howells' astonishment, Cahan told him he had read every line of his work and was his great admirer. They talked about literary matters, especially the Russian writers. In *A Hazard of New Fortunes* Howells had created a favorable socialist character, but his somewhat other-worldly Lindau could scarcely have prepared him for the passionate and knowledgeable Cahan. All in all, Cahan made a good impression on Howells.

They did not meet again until 1895, although the year before that Cahan had translated *A Traveler From Altruria* for his paper, a fact Howells learned about from his Jewish newsdealer. Their second meeting was a most important one. Mrs. Howells had picked up the copy of *Short Story* that contained "A Providential Match" and, recognizing Cahan's name, brought it home to her husband. Howells remembered the author and sent for him. He and Cahan talked at length; Howells did not think the story was "really a serious thing," but it convinced him Cahan must continue to write. He encouraged him to work up a more substantial piece on ghetto life. Cahan began almost at once on the manuscript of *Yekl.* When it was completed he sent it to Howells, who invited Cahan to come to dinner and talk about the novel. Cahan describes the atmosphere at dinner as follows:

> Howells' wife and daughter were at the table. In his house everything looked aristocratic in the American manner. The scent of spiritual nobility was in the air. Mrs. Howells held herself with American formality, but with American tact and true hospitality. (*Bleter,* IV, 34)

Afterwards, Howells praised the work, telling Cahan that "an important force had been added to American literature." He did not, however, like the title Cahan had given it—*Yankele the Yankee*—which he said was too much like vaudeville. He suggested the title that was accepted by Cahan, and by which the work became known in English: *Yekl: A Tale of the New York Ghetto.*

Then began the task of finding a publisher, something that proved more difficult than Cahan had anticipated. Howells was more philosophical than he about rejections, resigned to the fact that editors and publishers took into account market conditions when considering manuscripts for publication. To the contemporary reader, the grounds for rejection of *Yekl* by several prospective publishers are rather shocking, nevertheless, revealing the literary tone of the period and the obstacles which Realists like Cahan, Crane, even Howells, faced. In Cahan's case, the situation was made even more difficult by an at times scarcely concealed anti-Semitism.

The editor of *Harper's Weekly* returned the manuscript with the comment that "the life of an East-Side Jew wouldn't interest an American reader." Another (unnamed) rejected it in a note to Howells, saying,

> You know, dear Mr. Howells, that our readers want to have a novel about richly-dressed cavaliers and women, about women, about love which begins in the fields while they're playing golf. How can a novel about a Jewish immigrant, a blacksmith who became a tailor here, and whose wife is ignorant interest them?

Cahan went himself to pick up the rejected manuscript at the office of McClure's. "You portray only Jews," he was told by the editor. "According to your book one could believe that in America there are no other people but Jews." Cahan reported to Howells that this led to the following argument with the editor, John Sanburn Phillips:

> I cited examples from Russian literature, where in the

finest works the lives of poor and dirty peasants were described.

"Yes, but around these peasants are beautiful fields, and
grand meadows and forests," he pointed out.

"Do you think that a flower is more beautiful than the
beautiful soul of a peasant?" I asked.

"Does your Yekl have a beautiful soul?" Phillips asked.

In his own way, Phillips tried to encourage me. He said I
had a talent and suggested that I use this talent for Art, which
meant I should write about beautiful things.

He speaks like a wild man. . . . In Russia there would never
be such an editor. (*Bleter,* IV, 39–40)

Discouraged by all this, Cahan impatiently translated the story into Yiddish and began printing it in his paper, as *Yankele
the Yankee.* When Howells, who was still trying to find a publisher, found out about this publication, he was momentarily
distressed, but concluded with a smile that publishing in Yiddish meant "that the book hasn't been published." His remark
is reported by Cahan without comment, but it could only re-
inforce the conviction that a real literary career meant writing
in English. Finally, Howells succeeded in placing it with Appleton, and it appeared in due course in 1896.

Thereupon Howells gave it a rave review on the front page of
the *New York World's* fiction page, coupling it with a review of
Stephen Crane's *George's Mother.* The sub-title of the article is
of course an editor's work, but it is worth repeating in full:
"The Great Novelist Hails Abraham Cahan, the Author of 'Yekl,'
as a New Star of Realism, and Says that He and Stephen Crane
Have Drawn the Truest Pictures of East Side Life." In the article
itself, Howells notes that both writers are intensely realistic,
moved by the same artistic principle; Cahan, however, has more
humor and presents material that "makes a stronger appeal to
the reader's fancy." He goes on to say of Cahan,

I cannot help thinking that we have in him a writer of foreign
birth who will do honor to American letters, as Boyesen did.
He is already thoroughly naturalized to our point of view; he
sees things with American eyes, and he brings in aid of his

vision the far and rich perception of his Hebraic race; while he is strictly of the great and true Russian principles in literary art. . . . *Yekl* is, in fact, a charming book.

Howells always retained his admiration for Cahan—he reviewed his next book, *The Imported Bridegroom,* very favorably and included Cahan with a list of significant New York writers in a turn-of-the-century piece for English readers.[3] Years later, he had reservations about *David Levinsky* because of the focus on sensual matters in it, but it was a mild caveat at the end of Howells' long life. In the face of his obvious support of Cahan it may seem ungracious to ask if there was more involved for Howells than the simple championing of another realistic writer of talent. Such a motivation might be sufficient unto itself, but the terms of Howells' praise of *Yekl* as the work of a writer "naturalized to our point of view," who "sees things with American eyes," does raise some interesting questions about underlying cultural realities at stake in their relationship.

First of all, we must take a long step back and begin to see Howells' role in the late 1880s and through the '90s somewhat more analytically and critically than has usually been the case. The traditional picture of Howells' development is that after the Haymarket Affair in 1886 his social awareness deepened. Thereafter his life and work turned increasingly towards social issues, and in the process he encouraged many younger Realists (Henry Fuller, Stephen Crane, Charles Chesnutt, Frank Norris, Cahan) who were writing about the less "smiling aspects" of American life during this period of acute social change. By and large this portrait seems to me a true one, although it must be severely qualified with an awareness of Howells' deep ambivalences in this period and throughout his life.

This ambivalence concerned the matters of class, culture, privilege. Indeed, an important recent study indicts the entire notion of a so-called "renaissance" in Howells' social thinking during this period as being "as ephemeral as his sensitivity for the poor and the Jews was shallow."[4] This may be too strong a judgment, but it is true that from his earliest days in Boston, as Kermit Vanderbilt has shown, there was an essential contradic-

tion in Howells' value structure, as discerned in his attitude towards the poor, immigrants, Jews and Irish. He had a need, on
the one hand, as a midwestern commoner (from the perspective
of New England, his Ohio origins qualified him as a midwestern-
er), to champion a democratic ethos. Such an ethos sanctioned
his own rise in elite Boston, for it maintained that anyone of
talent could be embraced by the official culture. On the other
hand, once one has entered the charmed circle, there is the impulse to insist upon the superiority of the elites, which implies
a disdain for other rising groups, such as the Irish and Jews, so
that the rise would be stabilized and be seen to *mean* something.
As Vanderbilt shows, this kind of ambivalence is central to and
illuminates certain revisions and cruxes in that very important
novel by Howells, *The Rise of Silas Lapham.*[5]

It can be argued, therefore, that Howells was often impelled
by contradictory impulses and by strategies for evading their
true import and consequences. His brand of Realism, his usual
politics—to take nothing away from his bravery at the time of
Haymarket, when he alone among major American writers de-
fended the Anarchists—his very style, seem to me a compromise,
an effort to minimize these conflicts in his life. Basically, as Ziff
notes, Howells "was of the establishment, yet keenly aware of
its shortcomings."[6] He accepted his role as spokesman of the
intelligent middle-class, which he would try to educate—in one
way, by encouraging other writers more at home in this era of
perplexing social issues. In this period of his enlarged social
awareness Howells was essentially a mediator—just as he had
been earlier in his friendship and encouragement of those two
so dissimilar American writers, Mark Twain and Henry James.
Howells did heroic and priceless work in using his position to
introduce fresh, dissident talent to frequently indifferent or
Philistine audiences—as we have seen in his furthering Cahan's
early work—but the process of mediation and accommodation
worked both ways. He could not support writers who at some
point threatened *all* the assumptions of the class he represented.
In such a context his relations with Cahan can be better understood.

Thus Howells must have been favorably disposed to welcome
Cahan as a representative of the mysterious, swarming foreign
masses. Cahan, after all, revealed upon their first meeting that
he had read every line Howells had written and was "an inspired
reader and follower." Furthermore, despite his considerable
achievements, Cahan knew his experience was parochial, and he
was properly respectful of American culture and cultivation—as
his comments upon dinner at the Howells's show. Cahan, on his
part, was no fawning sycophant. He valued his own superior
grasp of the Russians and of socialist theory, but he had always
had a keen and unerring appreciation of Howells' unusual virtues
(as well as his limitations) as a Realist writer. He warmly appreciated Howells' kind human qualities—although there is no evidence they met again after *Yekl*—calling him a "dimentener
mentsch" (a diamond of a man) in his *Forward* obituary piece
when Howells died.

In his review of *Yekl*, Howells asked, "What will be the final
language spoken by the New Yorker?" It is a patently cultural
question that doubtless conceals a certain uneasiness. New York
will clearly become the dominant literary and cultural center of
the nation—Howells' own move from Boston in the late 1880s
was a sign of that. A question about its essential future qualities,
therefore, was really to ask what was in store for the American
culture. The question might be posed more boldly as, will it be
controlled and dominated by the new immigrants? Howells
touches urbanely on the possibility:

> We shall always write and print a sort of literary English, I
> suppose, but with a mixture of races the spoken tongue may
> be a thing composite and strange beyond our present knowl-
> edge. Mr. Abraham Cahan, in his "Yekl, A Story [*sic,* it
> should be "Tale"] of the New York Ghetto" (Appleton's), is
> full of indirect suggestions upon this point. Perhaps we shall
> have a New York jargon which shall be to English what the
> native Yiddish of his characters is to Hebrew, and it will be
> interlarded with Russian, Polish and German words, as their
> present jargon is with English vocables and with American
> slang.

Parenthetically, one might note that some few years after this, in *The American Scene* (1905), reflecting upon a visit to the East Side in the company of a leading Yiddish playwright (Jacob Gordin), Henry James would, in his inimitable way, draw out the anguished implications for "high culture" in such a state of affairs—the creation of a new kind of public, and a new language, by these new immigrants. He was not able to observe it as dispassionately as Howells presumably had. James:

> ... in these haunts of comparative civility we saw the mob sifted and strained, and the exasperation was the sharper, no doubt, because what the process had left more visible was just the various possibilities of the waiting spring of intelligence [i.e., here was no lump of people passively accepting notions of their intellectual inferiority, because they had not mastered the King's English]. Such elements constituted the germ of a "public" and it was impossible (possessed of a sensibility worth speaking of) to be exposed to them without feeling how new a thing under the sun the resulting public would be. That was where one's "lettered" anguish came in—in the turn of one's eye from face to face for some betrayal of a prehensile hook for the linguistic tradition as one had known it.[7]

James was not so sanguine as Howells—but then he did not have before him Cahan's *Yekl,* in which Howells saw many features that rendered his questions about the future of the culture rather rhetorical. Cahan's treatment of the immigrant problem in this work—as largely one of the immigrant's accommodation to American values, rather than of his impact upon those values —was basically reassuring to someone like Howells. Howells says at the very end of the review, as if in answer to the question he had posed at its beginning "I had almost forgotten to speak of his English. In its simplicity and its purity, as the English of a man born to write Russian [*sic,* Cahan was "born to write Yiddish"] it is simply marvelous." Reassured himself, Howells reassures his reader, in effect, that Cahan really is "one of us"; the center holds.

Predictably enough Howells praises the language of the narrator, which completely envelops and is obviously superior in
every respect to the crude, painfully rendered immigrant's English. The narrator is capable of frequent conceptual formula-
tions "placing" the story in a wider historical context, unlike
the immigrant's language that is sharply set apart from it. For
example, in the love scene in Chapter 8 ("A Housetop Idyll")
the characters attempt to handle unfamiliar emotions with their
broken English and seem only touching and a little absurd. The
old language did not deal with such concepts as "love" while
the new one is grasped only in clichés; the result is a sense of
their acting out forces they cannot comprehend. When the characters speak in a third language, as it were, that of the native
Yiddish transposed into English, there is a hint of more inner
richness than their English suggests. In this, of course, lies the
poignancy of the immigrant generation, the theme beautifully
developed much later by Henry Roth in his classic of the 1930s,
Call It Sleep. None of this was picked up by Howells. For him
the tale is simply that of the transformation of the immigrant
Yekl to "Jake the Yankee," a process that involves his giving up
his old spiritual and religious values, dress, appearance, and the
casting off of his pious, simple old-world wife, while taking on,
as Howells puts it, "our smartness and vulgarity with an instinctive fitness for that degree of fellow citizenship." That something painful is going on in this Americanization process, even
for someone as callow as Jake, is movingly rendered in the con-
cluding sentences of the book:

> But the distance between him and the mayor's office [where
> Jake was going in order to marry his new wife and become
> thoroughly committed to the new American values] was
> dwindling fast. Each time the car came to a halt he wished
> the pause could be prolonged indefinitely; and when it re-
> sumed its progress, the violent lurch it gave was accompanied
> by a corresponding sensation in his heart. (190)

It did not matter that this note in the book was not emphasized—the reading public was not especially interested in either

its pathos or its charm. Howells' review made a great difference to Cahan personally in that he was immediately accepted as a serious writer, became for a while a celebrity, but, as John Higham notes, "*Yekl* sold poorly and was soon forgotten despite Howells' promotion."[8]

About Howells, Cahan's last published comment, so far as I know, is the following: "I believe that Howells is today [c. 1927] one of the two most important writers in all of American literature. His main fault was his mildness and puritanic chastity. He was no fighter. He was unable to oppose the half-religious, unofficial but still powerful laws of morality. He always feared lest something indecent flow from his pen.

"He was an extremely soft man, good-hearted, tender. That was a hindrance to his art. However, there were great qualities in his writing. He created real people, 'Americans of flesh and blood' " (*Bleter,* IV, 23). The judgment is admiring, fair, and acute in its understanding of Howells' limitations. One feels in the end a certain unbridged distance between the worlds of the two writers.

CHAPTER FIVE

Jewish Immigrant Life in Early Stories

A Jewish Sensibility in American Letters

Among the putative young writers Lincoln Steffens had hired on the *Commercial Advertiser,* Cahan was something of a celebrity—keenly intellectual, he was older than most of them, possessed of varied experience, above all he was already *published.* After the critical success of *Yekl,* Cahan made serious efforts to develop his position as a literary figure. During his four years on the *Advertiser,* in addition to his prolific journalism, he published eight stories in leading periodicals, combined two of them with his two earliest English stories and a long new one in a volume called *The Imported Bridegroom and Other Stories* (1898), and planned a major novel on the immigrant experience. The novel was called *The Chasm,* a title symbolic of the cleft between Cahan's various worlds—Old and New, Talmudic and mod modern, Jewish and American. The work was warmly anticipated in literary circles, but it was never completed, nor has any part of it yet been located. One can only speculate that the chasm was wider than Cahan had sometimes thought and to bridge it more difficult than he expected.

There was obviously a need for someone in his mediating position between cultures, able to explain one to the other, en-

courage the best elements of one upon the other. There was
first of all the matter of Jewish and American cultures and their
relation to each other. Jews who felt chagrined at the unflatter-
ing portraits of Jake and Mamie in *Yekl*—understandably defen-
sive in an era of anti-Semitic stereotyping—could welcome his
sympathetic portrayal of the Jewish ethos in "The Russian Jew
in the United States," a long, thoughtful essay Cahan wrote for
the *Atlantic* in 1898.[1] From that essay, Gentile readers would
learn that Jews make good American citizens— they were literate, sober and hard-working, valued learning and spiritual values.
This position was a blow at those who thought Jews, like many
other groups in the "new immigration," were unassimilable—a
racist notion that hardened into law in the 1924 immigration
act that imposed discriminatory quotas on Mediterranean and
East European peoples. In his time, Cahan thus performed a valuable service in the cause of liberal enlightenment. He served
the same cause, frequently, although more obliquely, in the
stories he wrote during this period.

Similarly, Cahan played a progressive role in the literary culture of his time. Despite those editors who scorned the "sordid"
realism of *Yekl* and the people Cahan wrote about, his stories
continued in that vein and were welcomed by more discerning
editors. The stories encouraged readers and writers to honor
work that tried to deal honestly with ordinary people, of a type
frequently unknown to mainstream Americans. He tried to
bring the spirit of Tolstoy and Chekhov and of his East Side reporting into American literature—just as he was later to bring
the liberal spirit of the *Advertiser* to the world of Jewish radical
journalism. It was a perhaps impossible undertaking. Possibly
Cahan simply lacked the talent for such an ambitious synthesis
at this stage of his career—but the stories written between 1897
and 1901 show him getting deeper into the material—and its
difficulties. He moves from exploring the socially interesting
surface of immigrant life to sounding its psychological and spiritual tensions.

These thematic concerns are parallelled by structural and
tonal elements that warrant close scrunity. Although Cahan's
stories were aimed at an American audience—thus the filling in

of details about arcane Jewry, to the extent at times of providing footnotes about foreign words and customs—there is a sense
in which he never shook loose from his Yiddish journalistic self.
Perhaps unconsciously, one side of Cahan often addresses a Jewish reader—whose "thrill of truth" might come from recognizing
experiences unknown to Americans. Unless this point-of-view is
understood certain technical strategies will be misconstrued. For
a Jewish reader with the *shtetl* world behind him, the mere
mention of a fierce stepmother as the reason why a Jewish girl
embarks on a marriage with a Polish boy is sufficient to set a
tale going—in this case "The Apostate of Chego-Chegg," a story
to be considered in the next chapter. Such a reader, too, would
feel the full weight of mortification when a fellow Jew, with a
deceptively deferential politeness, refused to eat the food of a
meshumedste (apostate), and would believe wholly in the inerad-
icable alienation of spirit caused by conversion. All these are
givens, unquestioned assumptions of the tribe, sanctioned and
mythified orally and in literature through centuries. What might
at first seem a thinness of technique should be seen for what it
frequently is—the tentative introduction of a Yiddish sensibility
into American letters.

In our time, Isaac Bashevis Singer's work (first published in
the *Forward* by Cahan in the 1930s) is steeped in this kind of
sensibility and knowledge. Many of Bernard Malamud's stories,
as well, depend for their full effect upon the same assumptions.
That this is true in the work of these two writers seems to me
obvious. Less obviously, but I believe as cogently, there is Philip
Roth's Alexander Portnoy, whose complaints, however much
they represent the experience of other American boys growing
up in the '40s and '50s, must echo in special chambers of consciousness for Jews. When the Yiddish *knaytch* (style, tone,
twist) enters American literature, it comes through Abraham Cahan—tentatively, ambiguously, perhaps, but *there.* In addition
to his other contributions, therefore, he may be considered the
father of Jewish-American writers. Many of our finest contemporary writers attempt like him to hold in creative suspension a
sensibility attuned to Jewish life, the native American ground,
and a rich European tradition.

Ghetto Types and Situations

First now, a consideration of *The Imported Bridegroom,* the collection of five stories that deal largely with situations illustrating social realities in Jewish-American ghetto life. All the stories in the volume—which was well-received by Howells and other critics—display the same basic dynamic as *Yekl*: the impact of American culture on Jewish immigrants, but the range of personalities, types, occupations depicted is significantly broadened. The stories concern shopworkers, peddlers, boarders, intellectuals and former intellectuals (in two of the stories written after the more narrowly conceived *Yekl*), Talmudists and converted Talmudists, "shisters become misters" (and vice-versa), couples and would-be couples. The staple situations of much Yiddish and early Jewish-American literature are staked out by Cahan: synagogue life, graveyard visits and lamentations, weddings (interestingly enough, there are no childbirths in this collection), arrivals in the New World, visits back to the old village.

Two stories in the collection, "A Providential Match" and "A Sweatshop Romance," were written before *Yekl* and have already been discussed as forerunners of that book. The others are called "Circumstances," "A Ghetto Wedding," and "The Imported Bridegroom." In the following discussion of these three stories, most emphasis will be placed upon the long title story, which was written especially for the collection (all the others appeared previously in periodicals) and represents a kind of high point of Cahan's abilities at the time. It also is most revealing of his limitations.

Short and economical, "Circumstances" (which appeared initially in *Cosmopolitan* [22 April, 1897]) seems to me the best-realized work in the book. It is about a Russian-Jewish intellectual couple, Tatyana (Tanya) Markova and Boris Lurie, whose marriage and intellectual aspirations disintegrate under the brutal impact of their harsh economic situation in New York.

The story opens with Tatyana in a flurry of excitement because a new issue of a literary journal, *Russian Thought,* has arrived. She yearns to share its interesting contents with her hus-

band when he returns to their small apartment from his day's
work. Boris had been one of the best-read and most spirited
young men at the University in Kiev, but they had left Russia,
outraged when he had been told that "the way to the bar lay
through the baptismal font." Now he is fatigued at the end of
a day's work in a button factory, and so concerned about
their bare economic survival, that he cannot muster much enthusiasm for the "interesting points" she finds in the piece on
Maupassant.

It's a slack season, and in order to make ends meet, Boris proposes to Tanya that they do what other workingmen's families
do—take in a border. She is horrified at the idea, although Boris
hopes by it to raise enough money to enroll in a college. Ultimately, when he is laid off for two weeks and their situation
worsens, she agrees to accept as a boarder Dalsky, a friend and
former classmate of Boris's. The situation works out better than
either had thought. Dalsky is an orderly, serious medical student,
a welcome diversion for both of them. Inevitably, perhaps, the
contrast between the neat, purposeful collegian and Boris the
worker—no longer capable of study, careless of his appearance
and manners—produces in Tanya an awareness of love for Dalsky (aided by a reading of *Anna Karenina*). Nothing is said, but
Dalsky perceives the situation and arranges to move out. Boris
and Tanya are shattered by this turn of events. Unable to get
Dalsky out of her mind, Tanya finally leaves Boris. She writes
out for him—in his presence—the reasons for her action in an
impassioned but lucid statement. The story concludes a short
while later with scenes of Tanya and Boris separated and miserable. She is learning to operate a sewing machine in Silberman's
shop where "everybody and everything about her was so strange,
so hideously hostile, so exile-like." Boris returns from work to
the now completely empty apartment that he had shared with
Tanya, and as his loss sinks in, he weeps bitterly, crying out,
"Tanychka! Tanychka!"

The story focuses on types known to Cahan and in some ways
more challenging, in their closeness to his own situation, than
Yekl or Rouvke Arbel (of "A Providential Match"). Tanya is a
barishnaya, much like Cahan's own wife—that is, an idealistic,

well-educated, sensitive Russian woman. Her standards are in-
spiring, and there is a sweetness and delicacy in Cahan's portrayal of her thought processes, her excitement about literature, her
general spirit. All of these estimable qualities are undercut by
the pragmatic necessities of American life. Insofar as they are,
the story is a critique of this new life. But the author is balanced and objective, for it is difficult to conclude, finally, that
America's harsh economic exigencies present a worse choice
than Russian anti-Semitism. It is, at best, of course, an ironic
and highly qualified affirmation of America. Similarly, there are
two sides to Boris's accusation that Tanya's aristocratic preten-
sions are completely misplaced in their impoverished circumstances. Certainly the assertion is true enough, but immeasurably sad in its truth. As Tanya bends, alien and humbled, to her
work at the machine—not "the only Russian college woman to
work in an American factory"—and Boris weeps at his losses,
the denouement is effective and moving. Cahan achieves just the
right tone (what a wonderfully ironic touch to have Tanya *write
out* her reasons for leaving Boris—literary and a student to the
last!) of wry compassion at the end and throughout the story,
avoiding either sentiment or condescension.

I am not sure he achieves any such balanced control of complex emotions in the next story in the collection, although he
touches something subtle and rare in its ending. In "A Ghetto
Wedding" (published originally in *Atlantic* no. 81 [February,
1898]), a poor couple do not receive the gifts they expect after
investing all of their money in an expensive wedding, but find
solace in each other's love. A summary of this simple tale is
quickly given:

Goldie refuses to marry Nathan until they can save enough
money to have the kind of affair she considers proper: two carriages to drive them to the hall and back, and at least two hundred guests. As their savings dwindle during a slack work period,
she agrees to something less grand. She does convince Nathan,
however, that a large wedding will still in a sense repay itself.
They invest all the money they have left in a large wedding party for one hundred and fifty guests, counting on their gifts of
cash and house furnishings to repay their efforts. But most of

their acquaintances are suffering from underemployment, too, so that only some twenty guests appear at the wedding party and the gifts are shabby and sparse, far short of furnishing any kind of apartment. Goldie and Nathan walk back from their miserable wedding to the new apartment, through desolate and impoverished streets, enduring the mockery of a rough gang of Gentiles loitering in front of a saloon. Despite it all, they suddenly feel blissful and united, "the very notion of a relentless void abruptly turned to a beatific sense of their own seclusion, of their being only themselves in the universe to live and delight each other" (256).

Much of the story is contrived in situation and dialogue, predictable in plot. There is condescension towards the characters; the ending may seem sentimental. Yet the conclusion strikes a note that is beautiful—the sweetness and wonder of Chagall, an anticipation of Malamud. It is a note not always heard or appreciated in Cahan's work, but it is unmistakably there.

A much more substantial story, the longest and most complex in the collection, is the title-piece, "The Imported Bridegroom." The bridegroom referred to is a learned young Talmudist brought to America from his home village by a retired New York businessman (Asriel Stroon) for his daughter Flora. She is a determinedly "modern" girl, however, and refuses to marry the prodigy until he casts off his religious ways. The young man, Shaya, eventually becomes a thoroughly secularized intellectual, to the dismay of his father-in-law, and marries Flora. Her triumph is an ambiguous one, for she senses that Shaya has grown intellectually beyond her. It is a lovely and ironic story, wide-ranging and detailed in its execution, in its sophistication the appropriate climax of Cahan's work up to 1898. An extended summary and discussion will underscore these points.

Asriel Stroon is a widower of fifty-five and the father of a marriageable daughter when he makes a sentimental trip back to the Polish village of his birth. In retirement Stroon has had a religious awakening, and he considers this place, Pravly, the true seat of piety and genuine religious concern. While in the synagogue in Pravly he sees Shaya, an attractive young man who is a prodigy of Talmudic learning. The town's leading citizen has offered Shaya a large dowry in behalf of his daughter, which incites Stroon—who had previously lost to this citizen in bidding for synagogue honors—to offer Shaya an even greater dowry. He is determined to bring him back to New York as the groom of his unsuspecting daughter Flora.

Flora is quite Americanized (in a genteel way) and is not likely to consent to a match simply on her father's wish. She is a reader of Dickens, Thackeray and Scott, and has her heart set on marrying a physician and moving "uptown," away from their East Side dwelling. When her father returns from his trip with Shaya and confesses his hopes to her, she is amazed and indignant, but finally amused. She consents to allow Shaya to live in their house and pursue those religious studies that give her father and their old housekeeper Tamara such pleasure to participate in vicariously (both are basically simple, uneducated folk). Gradually Shaya learns English with the help of a teacher provided by Asriel, who delights in the feats of learning Shaya displays in the local synagogues. Flora begins to take a sisterly interest in this earnest and obviously very intelligent young man; she, too, helps him with his English.

Shaya discovers the Astor Library and the world of Gentile learning, which he finds an exciting challenge to his restless intelligence; he soon outstrips Flora in knowledge. Bending over a book together one day, they realize they are in love. Flora plans a deception—while pretending to continue his religious studies, Shaya will actually be training to become "a college boy" and ultimately a physician. He agrees to the plan and the young couple announce their betrothal to the delighted Asriel. Several months later, to his horror, Asriel discovers that instead of attending the various synagogues in the area Shaya has been constantly in the company of his previously discharged teacher of secular subjects. Furthermore, he has been seen going to the Astor Library and indulging in such blasphemies against the law as smoking cigarettes on the Sabbath. When Asriel secretly follows Shaya one day and actually sees him eating in a non-kosher restaurant, he is shaken to his roots. He confronts Shaya and denounces him as an *appikoros* (a heretic) and henceforth considers him dead to himself and Flora.

When he so informs Flora, she protests and rushes out to join Shaya. They are married forthwith in a civil ceremony at City Hall. When she tells her father this, he relents somewhat, and arranges to have a traditional Jewish ceremony performed. Nevertheless, Asriel's life in America now seems to him dark and empty ("America is now *treife* [unclean] to me") and in order, as he says, to be born again, he proposes to Tamara that after his daughter's wedding they marry and leave for Palestine, where they will end their days. Flora goes to tell Shaya the good news, only to find that he has gone out with his teacher friend. When he finally does return and she tells him of her father's assent to their marriage he is pleased, but asks to delay their meeting with him. He takes her instead to a smoky, crowded attic room, where a diverse group of Russian, American, Jewish intellectuals are engaged in an intense study and discussion of a book on the Positivist August Comte. The story ends with Shaya's absorption in the text before him, while Flora feels excluded from the alien gathering and Shaya's future.

The ending presents a neat surprise, and one in keeping with a ghetto reality. When the ideas of the west penetrated the Jewish communities of Eastern Europe towards the end of the nineteenth century they produced a ferment that shook loose many intellectually aspiring young people from traditional Jewish learning. Cahan understood the process well from his personal experience. He and others like him were propelled into secular modernism with a burst of pent-up energy. Jews accustomed to expend intellectual élan in the disciplined study of Talmud—which many of those in the movement towards enlightenment saw as an essentially medieval and scholastic task—now, as the broader world of thought opened to them, expended the same vitality upon social theories, science, literature, art, philosophy. Shaya's career illustrates a process familiar to many—the prodigious intellectual effort to bridge in a lifetime the gap from the Middle Ages to the modern world.

Cahan's portrayal of Shaya converted to the delights of Western thought, transferring the Talmudic study method of *pilpul* (dialectic argument) to his new subjects and surroundings is rooted, therefore, in a reality of the period. The first sight of New York from shipboard dazzles Shaya, and troubles the traditional elements in his vision:

> Can there be anything more beautiful, more sublime, and more uplifting than the view, on a clear summer morning, of New York harbor from an approaching ship? Shaya saw in the enchanting effect of sea, verdure, and sky a new version of his visions of paradise, where, ensconced behind luxuriant foliage, the righteous—venerable old men with silvery beards —were nodding and swaying over goldbound tomes of the Talmud. Yet, overborne with its looming grandeur, his heart grew heavy with suspense, and he clung close to Asriel. (47)

Such ambivalent feelings were inevitable and constant among immigrants. As we have seen, in this story Shaya moves away from Asriel and his traditionalism; and for venerable sages swaying over volumes of Talmud he substitutes in his American paradise intense intellectuals poring over volumes of the latest in advanced thought. It was a substitution often made.

There are many other authentic and shrewd touches. Flora's upwardly aspiring and shallow gentility rings true: the proud owner of a piano (which she played glibly) and a small library, the only one in her set to read Dickens, *et al,* "she was burning to be a doctor's wife." Her father wanted only a God-fearing business-man for her, the sort of man that girls in Flora's set normally married, not someone "deep in Gentile lore." But Flora's image of felicity was of "a more refined atmosphere than her own, and the vague ideal she had was an educated American gentleman, like those who lived uptown" (3). That her desire was as essentially bourgeois as her father's—who is, however, more sympathetic than she in his rough-hewn, bluff manner—and at the root as vulgar, Cahan leaves to be inferred from this speech at the moment of her commitment to Shaya:

> "Well, I want you to be a doctor, Shayie," she resumed with matronly tenderness. "If you are, I'll care for you, and

you'll be my birdie boy, an' all; if not, you won't. Oh won't it be lovely when everybody knows that you go to college and study together with nice, educated up-town fellows! We would go to theatres together and read different books. You'll make a daisy of a college boy, too—you bet. Would you like to wear a high hat, and spec's, and ride in a buggy, with a little nigger for a driver?—would you, would you, bad boy, you? Hello Doctor Golub! How are you?"

She presented her lips, and they kissed again and again. (82–83)

No doubt her sexual excitement was aroused as much by her image of that high-hatted doctor being driven by "a little nigger" (how disgustingly Americanized she was!) as by Shaya's presence. Her frustration at the end, when Shaya is launched on a path that probably did not include these worldly evidences of success and standing, must have pleased some malicious impulse of Cahan. After all, he coined the faintly contemptuous, anti-bourgeois term "allrightnik."

Much of the story and most of its vivid moments concern Asriel Stroon. The best scenes are those of Asriel back in Pravly. Cahan skillfully portrays Stroon's alternating sense of wonder at the return to his origins with his sense of the meanness of the village. The return is a mythic moment, involving the interplay of childhood and maturity, past and present, the New World and and the Old. Stroon goes through many changes. "At one moment he felt as though he had strayed into another world; at another, he was seized with doubt as to his own identity" (15). At one moment he feels like a child again, but "then he relapses into the Mott Street landlord, and for a moment he is an utter stranger in his birthplace. Why he could buy it all up now! . . . There was a time when he was of the meanest hereabout. An overpowering sense of triumph surged in his breast" (19). When he attends the local synagogue he is given a place of honor at the eastern wall, whereas in his earlier days his place had been a mean one, near the door. Stroon bids strenuously for the right to read from the *sedra* (the weekly portion of the Bible)—a lively scene of the auction process is one of the more memorable parts of the story—but loses to Reb Lippe, the richest man in town. The decision against him is an unfair one, and he complains bitterly about it—much to the chagrin of the townspeople, who find his behavior boorish. At that point, a shrewder realism replaces his idealization of Pravly. "All the poetry of thirty-five years' separation had fled from it, leaving a heap of beggarly squalor. He felt as though he had never been away from the place, and was tired to death of it, and at the same time his heart contracted with homesickness for America" (32).

Determined to show off his financial superiority, he outbids Reb Lippe for Shaya. The day after that strenuous encounter, he visits the local cemetery. At the grave of his father and the rest of his family he pours out his heart-felt longing to be forgiven for being a boor, to be admitted to a sanctified life, for his father to intercede with "the Uppermost" in his behalf. Earlier in the story, there was a mildly satiric irony in Asriel's reference to "The Uppermost," when the narrator has him punctuate his meaning by "pointing to the ceiling." Now the graveyard has the desired cathartic effect upon him. He seems at last to have reconciled past and present: "he felt new-born. Pravly was again dear to his heart, although Flora and America drew him to them with more magnetism than ever" (45). After all, it was the inhabitants of the graves, the dead parents and others connected intimately with his Pravly life, who represented the past. These he could only carry in his heart—and he could do that in America as well as anywhere. There was no need to pine for contemporary Pravly, so he could return to his real present in America with equanimity. He leaves gifts for all of Pravly, returns to New York, and seems at last to have achieved an integrated life. Of course at the end he is undone again. The American reality, proceeding according to its own dynamic, unravels his presumed integration of past and present. Asriel requires a new rebirth—this time in Palestine.

Done with a light and often satiric touch—in such scenes as that of Asriel and the old East Side Talmudists mumbling over words they venerate but scarcely understand, or Asriel confronting Shaya with the fact that he is eating pork—"The Imported Bridegroom" resonates with much solid specification of the

tensions and pulls on a people caught up in a significant change in
in their destiny. Asriel's final act of leaving America for Palestine might now be seen as prophetic, hauntingly symbolic—as if
a certain kind of diaspora Jew would ultimately have to seek integration of personality in the ancient homeland. More than
likely Cahan only thought it was an appropriate place for the
disillusioned Asriel to withdraw to—out of this world, in a sense,
a place to go to die. History and the destiny of living Jews was
to be worked out in America.

Despite such challenging ideas beneath its light surface, and
its knowledgeable use of the materials of Jewish ghetto life, the
story finally seems thin. The chief difficulty is the lack of depth
and roundness in the characters. However much Cahan tries to
individualize them, they remain types, almost caricatures. Asriel's identifying tag-line "I am a boor . . . but"—by repetiton
becomes as tiresome as Yekl's "Dotsha kin' a man *I* am," and
as reductive. There is a good deal of rant in Asriel, which re-
duces him at times to a comic stock character; the story moves
too quickly, the people act suddenly, impulsively, melodramat-
ically. In some of the later stories discussed in the next section,
this kind of thing will matter less as Cahan yields surface plausi-
bility for the sake of deeper psychological and mythic truths.
And after those stories, in his creation of David Levinsky, Cahan
will succeed in blending the individual and the typical, the personal, social and mythic elements that make up his character.
In his early work, Cahan had an eye for individualizing touches,
and for the dialectical quality of human character and behavior,
but his chief interest lay in the social reality depicted.

CHAPTER SIX

"The Real Truth" in the Later Stories

Within a two year period after the appearance of *The Imported Bridegroom,* 1899 to 1901, Cahan published half a dozen new stories in leading periodicals. All but one or two of them, in my veiw, mark a significant advance over his earlier work. In these stories Cahan goes deeper into questions of personality and strikes more profoundly notes previously only suggested. He closes upon immigrant feelings of loss, displacement, the yearning for inner authenticity.

This shift in focus can be seen in many ways, not the least of which is the change in the language used by the immigrant characters. The reader is directed towards facets of the immigrant experience other than the crude striving for Americanization in Yekl's fractured English or Flora Stroon's affectation of a refined style. In the later stories the immigrant's Yiddish, translated into good English, bears the burden of the tale and leaves one with an enriched sense of character. America is certainly present, it is the reality in which the characters move and have their being, but in none of the stories to be discussed in this section does anyone—outcast, poor, or commercially successful—reveal any special anxiety to rise or climb to acceptance in American terms.

In the order and place of their publication, these uncollected stories are "The Apostate of Chego-Chegg" (*Century*, November 1899); "Rabbi Eliezer's Christmas," (*Scribner's*, December 1899); "The Daughter of Avrom Leib," (*Cosmopolitan*, May 1900); "A Marriage by Proxy: A Story of the City," (*Everybody's*, December 1900); "Dumitru and Sigrid," (*Cosmopolitan*, March 1901); "Tzinchadzi of the Catskills" (*Atlantic*, August 1901). Several of them are rather remarkable.[1]

From Within Jewish Life

In "The Apostate of Chego-Chegg," Michalina (née Rivka), the apostate of the title, makes several fateful decisions. The first is made before the story opens, when she decides to marry the Polish youth Wincas and converts to his religion. Now in America, she decides to leave him and go back to her sorely missed Jewish faith. At the end she decides she cannot abandon Wincas and returns to him. From this résumé it would seem to be a story of religious loyalties, and of course to a considerable extent it is. But it is also a New World fable and a challenging story technically considered.

All the shifts in the story are handled quickly, as if the author were more interested in making a point than in achieving fully realized character and motive. On that level, it might seem fictionally weak. Howells and James handled these things better —in their best work a leisurely narrative pace and formal design create a sense of amplitude of character that makes the smallest gesture or the grandest renunciation comprehensible within the created fictional world itself. If we hold Cahan's stories to that standard they will frequently seem crude, however colorful or socially interesting they may be. There is, however, another tradition of story-telling—one that is moral and didactic, the narrative focused swiftly on crucial moments, a Yiddish tradition that Cahan, the old proletarian *maggid*, frequently tapped. If that is understood we will better appreciate the achievement of this story. Some of the issues at stake in the effort to fuse two traditions will be seen in the following summary and discussion.

The opening sentence is fine: " 'So this is America, and I am a Jewess no longer!' brooded Michalina, as she looked at the stretch of vegetable gardens across the road from the threshold where she sat." This could suggest the ordinary Jewish concern that America tended to strip away most vestiges of traditional Judaism, but here the lament is to be taken literally—Cahan has taken the old fear of America to its extreme point, beyond the pale as it were. She is declaring not mere non-practice of the old rules (that could be rationalized) but the fact of conversion, the ultimate horror of Jews, in America as well as in Europe. Michalina married Wincas in reaction to a cruel stepmother, and has been in America only a few days. They live in a village on Long Island, one of a dozen such, surrounded by farms worked by Polish peasants. There are two Jewish settlements nearby, the villages of Greyton and Burkdale, where some tailoring contractors had moved their sweatshops after a New York strike.

Michalina is terribly lonesome on this day, "yearning for her Gentile husband and their common birthplace and . . . for her father's house and her Jewish past." She notices Rabbi Nehemiah, in Old World dress, walking on the road from Greyton to Burkdale. Michalina follows him and sees him mocked by the young boys of Burkdale. She is recognized as the *meshumedste* (apostate) and driven out of town.

In their mutual need, Michalina and Wincas cling to each other. She is repelled by his countrymen, who in turn mock her as "the Jew woman." Ultimately, she bears a child, whom she at first repudiates as a *"shikse"* (Gentile girl), but then comes to love dearly. Nehemiah reappears, now a clean-shaven peddler who has become a crusading atheist. "There are no Jews and no Gentiles, missus. This is America. All are noblemen here, and all are brothers—children of one mother—Nature, dear little missus." Although he preaches a doctrine that is strange to her, she welcomes his visits, glad to hear Yiddish spoken. Finally, he declares his love for her (he calls her Laura to his Petrarch), but she spurns these advances.

She begins to win a kind of acceptance in Burkdale. Along with Nehemiah, she fills a role needed by the community if it is to define itself: "Burkdale without an atheist and a convert seemed as impossible as it would have been without a marriage broker, synagogue, or a bath house." Nonetheless, even tentative friendships stop when it comes to eating her food. Michalina's efforts to play the Jewess fail also, when she finds she cannot complete the benediction over her Sabbath candles. She had begun to light these in her home out of yearning for the sanctity of a Jewish life.

From Nehemiah she learns that according to the Jewish faith her marriage has never really existed. This fact is confirmed for her by a Rabbi she consults in the city. He tells her:

> "The God of Israel is not in the habit of refunding one's money. Oh, no! Once a Jew, forever a Jew—that's the way he does business."

If she wants to she can simply leave her husband and marry a Jew.

The women of Burkdale buy tickets to London for her and Nehemiah, where they plan to marry and start life anew. On the day of her departure, however, Wincas returns from work early, a sense of foreboding having overtaken him that morning at the manner of Michalina's farewell. When she sees him wandering about "like a cow in search of her calf," she concludes with sobs that she cannot leave him. Amidst the curses of the Jewish women, and in full knowledge that she has chosen a difficult course, she returns to Wincas. As the door closes upon the apostate, the last words of the story belong to a scornful townswoman: " ' A *meshumedste* will be a *meshumedste*.' "

As has been said earlier, the transitions in the story are made abruptly, and the characters' motives are often opaque. What seems contrived, however, becomes suggestive instead, if the allegorical or symbolic elements of the tale are stressed.

The setting and place names are deliberately allegorical. An old world *shtetl*—complete with *shadchen, shul* (synagogue), *mikva* (ritual bath)—and its values is transplanted intact to an American pastoral landscape. Within this unlikely setting, Cahan makes a characteristically double-edged statement. To the Gentiles he demonstrates the strength of Jewish values. To discerning Jews he is saying, in effect, such values can only be maintained artificially, although acculturation is not an unmixed blessing.

The names of the villages strike one immediately. Burkdale is named after Madison Burke, the developer who built the town. Recalling the two great conservative spokesmen of the eighteenth century, the name is appropriate to this place of runaway shops and fossilized social forms. Greyton suggests a neutral or, at worst, a lifeless setting—much like the name Woodenton that Philip Roth gives to the suburban setting of his story, "Eli the Fanatic." Like Roth's story, Cahan's tale addresses itself to the question of the proper attitude for Jews in the American paradise to have towards the Jewish past. Cahan's story shows much that is good in the old ethos, some bad, and nothing much better to replace it.

Positively, there is the sense of community Michalina feels when she is close to the culture of her birth. Her house radiates serenity; the women are warm, helpful, sympathetic. But when she transgresses, there is the vindictiveness of their curses, the absoluteness of their denial. It is a harsh alternative, nor is it mitigated by the image of American values we glimpse in Nehemiah and the city Rabbi. Nehemiah is still an object of ridicule when he replaces his archaic values with the jargon of science and modernity; the Rabbi a charlatan as the language of commerce invades his religious advice.

Cahan is playing with, balancing, the tensions between old world and new, America and Europe. Instead of resolution there is ironic awareness. The last line of the story parodies the familiar phrase, "Once a Jew always a Jew"—an epithet that can be a curse, boast, or the punch-line of a joke, depending on the point-of-view of the speaker. Switching to a traditional Jewish view of conversion to foreign values, Cahan is subtly exposing his Christian readers to the wisdom known to every Jew in Christendom: that there are two answers, or ways, to see every question. The story ends on this ironic note, but suffusing it is Cahan's understanding of loneliness and of people's need to cling to one another in the darkness.

Cahan's next two stories are written from inside Jewish life—as signaled by their titles, "Rabbi Eliezer's Christmas" and "The Daughter of Avrom Leib"—with an eye, again, to informing sympathetically a Gentile audience. More than that, of course, goes on in the stories—complications in the Jew-Gentile relationship, and a sense of complexity in characters who speak from their inner selves.

Rabbi Eliezer runs a poor newsstand in a ghetto market. On Christmas Day, two Gentile women in search of local color are moved by the sight of this bearded patriarch and make him a gift of twenty dollars. At first overjoyed, Eliezer struggles with his conscience about accepting what may be a gift commemorating a Christian holiday. After much inner debate, he blurts out this fear to one of the women as he returns the gift. To his pleasure, she promises to give it back to him the day after Christmas.

This résumé suggests the anecdotal quality of the story, but does little justice to its economy, fine dialogue, sense of character. Eliezer's character is most subtly displayed at the end of the story as he vacillates between high spirits at the expectation that the money will be his again and shame that he should have attempted even in his thoughts to deceive his God. He blurts out a doleful prayer, murmuring about his unhappiness in a veritable "ecstasy of woe" while in the back of his mind there lurks the question "will the Gentile lady pay him the twenty dollars?"

Cahan's irony is gentle, but everywhere apparent in the story: in the slumming ladies, images of bourgeois condescension and incomprehension (they pick up two packs of cigarettes from Eliezer's stand, not recognizing the pictures of Dreyfus and Karl Marx on them); and in Eliezer himself, who is regarded as an art object by the ladies, but is as much *shlemiehl* as saint. Most striking, however, are the intimacy with which Eliezer's thought processes are caught, and the fine rhythms of speech in the ghetto characters. Cahan anticipates many later Jewish writers when he reproduces the sales pitch of a fish-peddler: " 'Fish, fish, living fish—buy fish, dear little housewives! Dancing, tumbling, wriggling, screaming fish in honor of the Sabbath! Potatoes as big as your fist! A bargain in muslin! Buy a calico remnant—cal-

ico as good as silk, sweet little housewives!' " In this same vein,
I must quote Eliezer's longest monologue in answer to questions
of the women (who are social workers). They ask how much his
stand brings him, about his bookcase and how his skills are
received in America:

"I sit freezing like a dog from six in the morning to eleven
in the night, as you see. And what do I get for my pains?
When I make five dollars I call it an extra good week. If I
had a larger stock I might make a little more. It's America,
not Russia. If one would do business one must have all kinds
of goods. But then it's a sin to grumble. I am not starving—
praised be the All High for that."

Speaking of his bookcase, he explained that it was a circulat-
ing library.

"Silly stuff that," he said with contempt. "Nothing but lies
—yarns about how a lad fell in love with a girl and such-like
nonsense. Yet I must keep this kind of trash. Ah, this is not
what I came to America for. Was I not happy at home? Did
I want for anything? Birds' milk, perhaps. I was a *sopher* [a
writer of parchment scrolls of the Pentateuch or some other
section of the Old Testament] . I was poor, but I never went
hungry, and people showed me respect. And so I lived in
peace until the black year brought to our town a man who
advised me to go to America. He saw me make a *Misrach*—a
kind of picture which pious Jews keep on the east wall of the
their best room. I fitted it up with beautiful pillars, two lions
supporting the tables of the Law and all kinds of trappings,
you know. Well, all this lots of people could do, but what no-
body could do and I can is to crowd the whole of Deuteronomy into a circle the size of a tea-glass." A sparkle came into
his dark brown eyes; an exalted smile played about his lips;
but, this only deepened the gloom of his face. "I would just
take a glass, stand it on the paper upside down, trace the brim
and—set to work. People could hardly read it—so tiny were
the letters; but I let everybody look at them through a mag-
nifying glass and they saw every word. And how well written!

Just like print. 'Well,' says that man, 'Rabbi Eliezer,' says he, 'you have hands of gold, but sense you have none. Why throw yourself away upon a sleepy town like this? Just you go to America, and pearls will be showered on you.' " After a little pause Rabbi Eliezer waved his hands at his wares and said, with a bitter smile: "Well, here they are, the pearls."

"And what became of your pictures?" asked Miss Colton.

"My pictures? Better don't ask about them, good lady," the old man answered, with a sigh. "I sat up nights to make one, and when it was finished I got one dollar for it, and that was a favor. My lions looked like potatoes, they said. 'As to your Deuteronomy—it isn't bad, but this is America, and such things are made by machine and sold five cents apiece.' The merchants showed me some such pictures. Well, the lions were rather better than mine, and the letters even smaller— that I won't deny—but do you know how they were made? By hand? Not a bit. They write big words and have them photographed by a tricky sort of thing which makes them a hundred times smaller than they are—do you understand? 'Ah, but that's machinework—a swindle,' says I, 'while I make every letter with my own hands, and my words are full of life.' 'Bother your hands and your words!' said the merchant. 'This isn't Russia,' says he. 'It's America, the land of machines and of "hurry up!" says he, and there you are!' " The old man's voice fell. "Making letters smaller, indeed!" he said, brokenly. "Me, too, they have made a hundred times smaller than I was. A pile of ashes they have made of me. A fine old age! Freezing like a dog, with no one to say a kind word to you," he concluded, trying to blink away his tears and to suppress the childlike quiver of his lips.

All of Cahan's knowledge of Jewish life informs this passage; and his skill as a writer endows it with warmth and wit. The attitude behind it is important: Cahan allows Eliezer's real language, the language of his inner life, to represent him fully. He simply ignores the implausibility of this kind of articulate communication in English by a man like Eliezer only two years in America. For the sake of a more significant truth, Cahan has moved away from the verisimilitude that tried to capture the dialect of immigrant English. The Misses Colton and Beamis see Eliezer as an exotic (sympathetically, to be sure); the man himself confronts the Gentile world of ladies with no sense of that at all, but as an equal, despite his poverty and difference, because of the rich, felt reality of his own experience.

In "The Daughter of Avrom Leib," Cahan uses the materials of the Jewish religious tradition more extensively than in any of his other works. The Jewish Sabbath and chief holidays, with the rituals, prayers, customs associated with them, provide the structure upon which the story is built. The whole is something of a tour-de-force. The story of the meeting, wooing, losing and winning of Sophie, daughter of Reb Leib, a pious and accomplished cantor, by the manufacturer Aaron Zalkin unfolds within a carefully structured framework based on the Jewish religious calendar and the most traditional aspects of its culture. The scheme affords Cahan the opportunity to inform the readers of *Cosmopolitan* in a dignified way about the elements of an arcane but obviously extremely rich and spiritual religion. At the same time, he explores some very modern aspects of character in Sophie and Zalkin.

The story is divided into eight sections, called "Welcoming the Bride," "Sabbath of Comfort Ye," "Yom Kippur Eve," "The Rejoicing of the Law," "Blessing the Dedication Lights," "Reb Avrom's Last Composition," "Days of Awe," and, finally, "Rejoicing of the Law Once More." In them, Cahan takes us into a synagogue on the Sabbath Eve, naming and explaining the prayers and rituals and the chief holidays on the Jewish religious calendar. There is the solemn Day of Atonement (*Yom Kippur*); the high-spirited celebration of the holiday called The Rejoicing of the Law (*Simchath Torah*); the holiday of the Maccabean Triumph when candles are lit and dedicated (*Chanukah*); and the preparation and celebration of the high holy Days of Awe (from *Rosh Hashonah* to *Yom Kippur*) which commemorate the advent of the New Year.

Each section also depicts another stage in the suit of Zalkin and Sophie. In the first, Aaron Zalkin, "a great feeling of loneliness" having taken hold of him, wanders down to the streets of

the ghetto and into a synagogue (for the first time in fifteen
years). There he listens to the cantor Reb Avrom Leib and is
charmed by him and his marriageable daughter Sophie, who is
among the congregation. In the second section, he remembers
the cantor and his daughter on the next Sabbath Eve and finds
himself once again in the synagogue. The synagogue song touches his heart; he sends a marriage agent to Reb Avrom Leib and
is introduced to the household. He and Sophie are at first disappointed in each other, but the old man falls in love with
Zalkin's suddenly revealed talent for Talmudic argument. As
Sophie plays her father's airs on the piano, Zalkin revels in the
familial warmth that has been absent since his childhood. He
proposes to Sophie, who, despite misgivings about his appearance, accepts him. Their betrothal is announced on the night of
the Sabbath of "comfort ye," a traditional time for such an-
nouncements (it comes immediately after a nine-day period of
mourning for the fall of the Temple). The old man is ecstatic,
but Sophie reflects sadly that when she marries, the old widower will be alone without her (although she has two teen-age
brothers).

In the next section, on the eve of the Day of Atonement,
when all sins must be confessed, Sophie tells Zalkin that "for a
day or two I had thoughts against you," and that once she had
cursed him in her mind. She asks his forgiveness, protesting her
love—but he is chilled by the thought that she had cursed him,
and apparently could not stand him. All during the services his
heart lies heavily in him; the next day he writes her "a long letter, full of open resentment and ill-disguised misery, declaring
their engagement off." He is soon miserable, however, and
changes his mind. Once again in the synagogue, during the celebration of the Law, he urges Sophie, through her father, to
wear again the engagement brooch he had given her earlier. The
old man orders her to take it back; to his great pleasure she
obeys. During the holiday festivities, Reb Avrom has meanwhile
caught a fatal chill. As the autumn approaches winter, Reb
Avrom's health continues to fail while Zalkin's suit does not
thrive with Sophie, who repulses his efforts at physical affection. By *Chanukah* their engagement is broken off once again.
The following July, Reb Avrom on his death-bed composes his

last air for the forthcoming high holidays. As the Days of Awe approach, Sophie tries to get other cantors in the ghetto to perform her dead father's final composition. It is a fruitless endeavor, since each cantor has his own material. The high holidays are inexpressibly sad for Sophie and her brothers without the vibrant, commanding presence of their father. In the final section, at the ceremony of rejoicing at the Law—the scene the previous year of her father's transports of joy—the tearful Sophie is confronted once again by Zalkin who finds he cannot live without her. He proposes again, and reminded of his affection for her father, Sophie accepts him. Will she really marry him this time? "Yes, yes," she says, the narrator adding, "And as if afraid lest morning might bring better counsel, she hastened to bind herself by adding, with a tremor in her voice: 'I swear by my father that I will.'"

This story could have been written by Malamud—especially the portions dealing with the impulsive vacillations of Sophie and Zalkin, searching for an emotional connection. Each is for the other obviously a surrogate only for something irrevocably lost. Zalkin's is an evocative portrait, the successful manufacturer haunted by loneliness and nostalgic for some vision of an earlier felicity. There is a distressing side to Zalkin's character; by turns callow and sentimental, self-pitying, he is in some respects an emotional cripple. We are told at one point that the compliments Zalkin offers to Sophie are the first he's ever paid any woman. Her suspicion of him would indeed seem to be justified. In all these respects, he is a forerunner of David Levinsky, whose loneliness is more profoundly articulated and less mitigated, finally, than Zalkin's. From the ambiguous tone of Sophie's last affirmation and her recoil at Zalkin's kisses earlier, it is doubtful that these two sufferers will relieve each other for long from a fundamental sense of a lost center in their lives. It is this suggestion, however steeped the tale may be in a venerable succouring tradition, that gives the story its modern resonance.

Other Immigrant Nationalities

In his next stories—"A Marriage by Proxy," "Dumitru and Sigrid," and "Tzinchadzi of the Catskills"—Cahan turns from tales of Jewish life, but still mines the immigrant experience. The theme of cultural and personal displacement is touched upon in these stories of Italian, Swedish, Circassian immigrants, but only in the last one, "Tzinchadzi of the Catskills," is it more than anecdotally treated.

"A Marriage By Proxy" is about an Italian barber who arranges a marriage by mail which at first does not work out, but then succeeds when the young bride is fooled into accepting him. It is almost a folk-tale, in an immigrant setting. More fully, the story is as follows.

Roberto, a barber in New York, arranges a marriage with Philomena by mail. She comes from Italy accompanied by Antonio, who has stood in for his brother Roberto in the wedding ceremony. When Philomena meets Roberto for the first time at Ellis Island, she is disappointed in his age and appearance. Months later, in a chance meeting with Antonio, the narrator hears the full story of subsequent developments. At first Philomena insisted on being sent home, or at least living apart from Roberto. He loves her, plies her with gifts and affection, but she spurns him. On the advice of an old matchmaker and fortune-teller whom Roberto finally consults in desperation, he stops sending her gifts and Antonio is bade to leave town. The old matron tells Philomena that her troubles will soon be over, since it has been arranged for Roberto to fall in love with his banker's daughter. Hearing that Roberto will now annul their marriage and gladly send her home, Philomena becomes jealous and possessive. She moves back to Roberto; within a few months they are in love and happy. When the narrator goes to Roberto's barber-shop he finds her contentedly taking cash, she being a good business woman now among the other virtues Roberto finds in her.

The story has a certain charm, but it is basically glib, none of the characters suggesting depth. It is noteworthy primarily because "A Marriage by Proxy" is the first English story by Cahan in which the narrator is a self-conscious "I"—an American reporter. His job is writing about immigrants coming to Ellis Island, a good source of "human interest" stories to which the "I" is warmly responsive. Cahan—or the narrator—is more clear-

ly and self-consciously "the American" in relation to these immigrants than in his stories of Jewish life.

"Dumitru and Sigrid" has the same anecdotal quality, although the theme of emotional displacement is more seriously
treated. It tells the story of a growing affection between two
immigrants from different countries, begun with the aid of a
dictionary, that is thwarted by the exigencies of their American
lives. The crippled communication of immigrants, revealed in
their language difficulties—once the mother tongue is lost, nothing can truly replace it—strikes a note central to Cahan's concerns. The story's origins include an anecdote Cahan tells in his
memoirs about learning English from the dictionary aboard
ship, and his later experience as a reporter on Ellis Island.

At the Barge Office on the Island, immigrants of all nationalities wait in a noisy babble for permission to enter the United
States. Some are merely awaiting relatives, some have lost an address, or have arrived penniless. One of the latter is Dumitru
Robescu, a young Rumanian, French-speaking and refined (he
was a former army officer), who was kept in Bremen longer
than he had expected and so used up his money. He cannot be
allowed into the country until employment is found for him.
While he waits in the "detention pen" for several days, he befriends Sigrid, a Swedish girl who has lost the address of her
aunt and must now wait until she is located. After a period of
dumb communication they begin, with great difficulty but increasing excitement, to communicate by writing in English—he
using a Rumanian-English dictionary, she a Swedish-English
one. In one of their last exchanges, he had said she was a "good
angel," to which she replied jokingly " 'And you bad man.' "
" 'I not joke, Sigrid,' " he then writes, " 'know not where I be
and where thou be, but I eternal remember thou.' " She replies,
" ' I also never forget thou. Never, never.' " Shortly thereafter,
they are separated: her aunt has come for her, and he receives
employment. His first months are heartbreakingly desolate; Sigrid is never absent from his daydreams. Along with his mother
and sister at home, she is the object of his most fervent yearnings for love and communion. His searches for Sigrid are fruitless.

His material condition improves. Some two and a half years after his arrival he is a successful and well-turned out photographer, on the whole "getting to like his new home" so well that he "went wild over every victory of American armies" during the Spanish war. Still, he "felt lonely, gnawingly lonely"—his mother by now dead and Sigrid still a dream. One day he encounters her by chance on the front steps of a new tenement house, with a baby in her lap. She is broader, but still comely. When he says " 'I do you do,' " she answers " 'I am ull righd, dang you . . . I didn't see you since ve vas dere (pointing in the direction of the Barge Office). I ulvays dought I vill see you sometimes.' " It is their first oral conversation. She then calls to her husband, and when he comes she explains to him, with a joyful laugh: " 'Dis is de gentleman vat mashed me in Castle Garden. I tol' you—you remember?' " Husband and wife smiled as at a good joke.

At this, Dumitru feels "like one listening to the scratching of a window pane" and he hastily departs. His cheeks are burning, he feels ridiculous. The next Sunday, when he goes to the Russian Church (where he does not understand the language, but it is as close to his own church as there is) and prays for the soul of his mother and the health of his sister, he omits to mention Sigrid for the first time.

As I have indicated, the subject is central to Cahan's serious concerns—the harshness of the immigrants' emotional condition is parallelled in the harshness and ugliness of the language they are forced to speak. The pathos of the situation is clear. We can feel the indignity of Dumitru when his most ardent and spiritual feelings are reduced by being described as "mashing." The tragedy of the immigrant is partly this near impossibility of total communication in a strange new tongue. An important part of a person is thereby isolated in emotional silence. Dumitru, a French-speaking Rumanian, given work by a German society, attending a Russian church, trained by a Frenchman and about to enter a partnership with a Czech, is almost a paradigm of this kind of displacement from a linguistic and cultural center (despite his newly acquired American patriotism). Interestingly enough, Dumitru's profession is the non-verbal one of photogra-

phy. The story is highly suggestive in these respects, and poignant certainly, but in its lack of fictive complexity it remains
only one step above the journalist's art.

In "Tzinchadzi of the Catskills," Cahan continues in a somewhat more ambitiously conceived story his rich view of this
kind of material. Tzinchadzi is a Circassian immigrant who succeeds as an American businessman, but who yearns unhappily
for his past self. The story's framework is again that of the interested, somewhat superior American narrator being told a
story by a more than faintly exotic immigrant. At the end, however, something more complicated emerges as a kinship between
the narrator and Tzinchadzi is subtly established.

A bored guest at a summer resort in the Catskills, the narrator's mood is enlivened by the surprising appearance one day of
a bearded horseman, all got up in turban, cassock, sword, dashing about on a white steed. It develops that this is Tzinchadzi,
a former Georgian nobleman, now a peddler of Circassian wares
in the resort area, enjoying himself in the traditional costumes
and manner of his country. The narrator searches him out
and since he knows Russian, Tzinchadzi is able to tell him about
his intense homesickness, and why he left his native land. It
seems he had loved and lost a lovely maid, in a manner that still
upsets him. A horsemanship contest had been held to determine
whether he or his rival, Azdek, should win the hand of Zelaya.
Tzinchadzi tells the narrator how he had performed so spectac-
ularly that Azdek was simply unable to compete and was loudly
jeered by the Circassians. Ironically, this earned him Zelaya's
pity. She had accused Tzinchadzi of being without a heart and
chose Azdek. In chagrin, Tzinchadzi left the country when he
was recruited by the American consul as a trick rider for the
1893 Chicago World's Fair. He decided to remain in America,
selling the wares of his country. As the narrator can see, Tzinchadzi continues, (bringing his tale up to the present), Americans like
his horsemanship, buy his goods, and he makes much money.
But he misses the Circassian mountains and still feels keenly the
loss of Zelaya. Tzinchadzi tells his story with many romantic
flourishes and a poeticized diction that is occasionally deflated
by a sardonic narrative intrusion (" 'How was the weather,' "

the narrator asks about the day of the contest), which emphasizes the distance between narrator and Tzinchadzi. Six years
later, however, the narrator meets him by chance on a New
York ferryboat and Tzinchadzi has changed dramatically. Gone
are his beard and colorful costume; he owns real estate and a
busy store. Americans find it hard to pronounce Tzinchadzi, so
he has changed his name to Jones. "He had grown fat and rud-
dy, he glistened with prosperity and prose," says the narrator.
In answer to the narrator's questions, Tzinchadzi-Jones says he
no longer bears Zelaya and Azdek a grudge, does not feel homesick, thinks America is a fine place. Suddenly he bursts out ve-
hemently with, as he says, "the real truth": that although he
has money and friends he is not happy, because he now yearns
" 'neither for my country, nor for Zelaya, nor for anything
else.' " He has concluded that a man cannot be happy without
something or someone to yearn for. He used to be in anguish,
but when he lost that pain, he lost his happiness. He now yearns
for . . . what? The narrator is about to reply ironically, " 'For
your old yearnings,' " but he decides this is too commonplace
for Jones's mood, and so he remains silent. The last words in
the story are these: " 'I have plenty of money; but if you want
to think of a happy man, think of Tzinchadzi of the Catskills,
not of Jones of New York.' "

This conclusion foreshadows *David Levinsky,* but more interesting is the narrator's silence as Tzinchadzi breaks out of the
narrative framework to have the last word. It would have been
easy to deflate his "yearning for yearning" as sentimental,
vague, pretentious. But the narrator has recognized a genuine
human emotion, one that suddenly touches him. It becomes
clear that the story is as much the narrator's as Tzinchadzi's.
The narrator at the beginning and throughout the story is precisely the kind of person Tzinchadzi has become at the end—
someone full of "prosperity and prose." On the crowded ferryboat, he describes himself "watching the splinters of a shattered
bar of sunshine on the water, and listening to the consumptive
notes of a negro's fiddle." His description refuses to sentimen-
talize nature or romanticize the colorful human scene before

him, but it seems sour, not merely objective and realistic. Accomplished and successful, he, too, has lost the capacity to "yearn." Bored at the beginning of the story, he is detached and strangely affectless at the end. The "real truth" blurted out by Tzinchadzi speaks for the narrator and all of Cahan's characters: no amount of successful adaptation to the material surface of American life can fulfill, finally, the pressing needs of the human soul.

CHAPTER SEVEN

A Yiddish Interlude

Neshomah Yeseroh

Cahan's stories in English combine, as we have seen, the elements of his Russian and Jewish experience within an American
framework—bringing news of other worlds, other sensibilities,
to his American readers. During the *Advertiser* years his essays
in American periodicals, as well, inform an English-reading public about Jewish and Russian life, Jewish and Russian authors.[1]
Towards the end of this period, Cahan was induced to write in
Yiddish again for the audience of the *Forward,* to help articulate for those readers some qualities of their American experience. The most notable difference from his English stories is
that the Yiddish work was scarcely to be considered "fiction"
and that in it Cahan was overtly the teacher and socialist.

Between November 1900 and January 1901 Cahan produced
a series of "articles" in Yiddish, later published in book form as
Neshomah Yeseroh, that tells a good deal about Cahan's socialism at the time, and about his more casual attitude towards
writing in Yiddish than in English. The series was only undertaken after much imploring by the editor of the *Forward,* the
busy Cahan hoping to find something in his notes that would
not take much effort to work up. Among his notes for "The
Imported Bridegroom" he found such an idea—a sketch for a

story that would involve a disappointment like Asriel Stroon's, but whose central character would be a socialist worker, not a successful and religious businessman.

An honest socialist worker, Cutler, has a daughter, Rachel, who marries another socialist (Harry). Cutler also has a son named Muzi whom he brings up in the true faith from childhood on. Harry and Rachel have a cheerful household—many guests come there, all socialists. The careers of Cutler and his family and some of their acquaintances are followed over many years. Harry owns a store that thrives; he becomes rich and abandons socialism. He and Rachel now see only two of the former comrades, both doctors and utterly in the grip of money-making. The old *neshomah yeseroh* (the transcendent spirit of idealism) is gone from them all. The Socialist Party itself is in the control of less admirable types than formerly and so has lost the respect of the masses. Muzi has gone to City College and grown away from his father. Cutler has kept the faith, but wanders about like a lost soul. His final tragedy occurs when he sneaks into a Tammany beefsteak party and hears his son make a speech for the local boss. Cutler shouts a protest and is thrown out. Ultimately, he becomes ill and dies. His name is not even commemorated in his comrades' newspaper, since he has not been a well-known writer or speaker. His survivors continue to ride in their carriages and to play poker.

Another story of the death of the spirit is told about a once virtuous man who became an important and corrupt saloon owner. America had made him a worse man than he had been formerly; of course there are instances of the opposite occurring. Circumstances can occasionally improve people, whose inner spirit enables them to act humanely.

The narrator recalls that in the first group of immigrants all were poor, all lived in one world, all were socialists. Now at New Year's two parties are held on the East Side: a socialist one at which beer is drunk; and one at which full-dress suits are worn, champagne is drunk, and socialist ideals are held in contempt. There are now two worlds where formerly there was one.

Finally, the narrator notes that the *neshomah yeseroh* does not discriminate between Jews and Christians. There can be an aristocracy of the spirit. The largest number of great men in the world are, after all, not Jews; but still, for their small numbers, Jews do have the greatest proportion of poets, singers, martyrs (he had spoken earlier of the Russians, especially the nihilists), good heads and good hearts. The time will come when we will all be united and the result will be a stronger and better mankind. On this note the story ends.

The work runs to over eighty pages, in nine sections, and betrays even in the summary above, the makeshift and structurally awkward quality to be expected from the circumstances of its composition. Cahan fleshed out his idea about the honest socialist worker—a later, sadder version of Rafael Naarizokh—with several other case histories and much commentary. Cutler does stand out; and the theme of disappointed expectations, paralleling the Asriel-Shaya story in "The Imported Bridegroom" is nicely handled, but even more than in the earlier story characterization is overwhelmed by narrative comment and moralizing.

Cahan knew his audience, however, and the series was a great success. *Neshomah yeseroh* is a Hebrew phrase, referring to the second soul that is supposed to descend on Jewish households on the Sabbath. It is a concept that has a great appeal for Cahan. Towards the end of the series he defines it as being like Emerson's "oversoul," so that a good translation of the phrase would be "The Transcendent Spirit." That spirit should inform all idealist aspirations and deeply humane relations. It is the spirit which should inform true socialism. Cahan's ethical idealism, the spiritual nature of his socialist commitment—and the rueful sense of its precariousness in the American reality—has rarely been better or more directly conveyed than in this work. "Neshomah yeseroh" was even praised by his then great adversary Jacob Gordin; but the best comment reported by Cahan was that "In the several years in which Cahan has been writing only English, his Yiddish has become better" (*Bleter,* IV, 251–54).

Fanny's Khasonim

The relation of the two languages and the different parts of his sensibility Cahan explored in each is vividly demonstrated in another work he undertook at this time. Cahan wrote an English draft of a long story called "Fanny and Her Suitors," which he hoped some day to polish and make the basis of a book. But he never found time to fulfill the plan. Instead, several years later he reworked it, translated it into Yiddish and published it as "Fanny's Khasonim" in a volume along with "Neshomah Yeseroh," where it appeared for the first time in 1913.[2]

"Fanny's Khasonim" is a third longer, and more unified than "Neshomah Yeseroh" but shows even more clearly the split between Cahan's Yiddish didacticism and his less tendentious English literary work. The novella of seven chapters that originally comprised "Fanny and Her Suitors" is included within a Prologue and Epilogue that are added for the Yiddish version. The additions introduce a socialist editor given to long speeches presenting the socialist line on love, marriage, the family, whereas the body of the tale allows Fanny, an ordinary shop worker, to tell her story in her own words.

The Prologue sketches an encounter in a park where Cahan (or, rather, an unnamed "I"—who is an editor) and several friends are having a discussion that draws a crowd around them. Among the listeners is a middle-aged woman who involves him in an intense conversation, wanting to know his—and generally the socialist—view of love, marriage, and related questions. She chooses good questions and interests him. She reveals that she has a manuscript at home, and though she is an uneducated and ordinary woman, a shop worker, it might be of some interest to others. She would like him to read it and then do what he pleases with it—throw it out, revise it, publish it. She brings it to him the next day. The editor reads it and decides it should be published just as she wrote it. The tale that follows purports to be this story in her own words, only slightly edited.

Fanny tells about a series of suitors she has had who have ultimately turned away from her, and about twice being in love. Through her tale she sprinkles reflections on being an "old maid," one who was "left," and upon men and women's relations—love and marriage—generally. Marriage has been urged upon her for many years, largely by her younger sister (who had run off in the old country with a deserting Jewish soldier) and her old mother—although the mother is in conflict since Fanny is her breadwinner. All of her popular sister's friends also enter into the sport of finding appropriate suitors for her. Fanny is under a great deal of pressure from them all, as she sees it, and from the community at large.

Fanny cannot hold any suitor's interest for long. Even one who had admired her good sense and steadiness and thought he was beyond romance finally sought out someone who could touch his heart. She believes that the root of her problem is, variously, that unlike her sister she simply does not radiate feminity, that she is only ordinary in appearance—neither beautiful nor ugly, she simply cannot attract attention to herself—or that she does not have a large enough dowry (from which she concludes that money in itself is the source of all evil). The men she meets are not always entirely attractive types, either. But the double standard of morality places them under less pressure to marry and, in any case, they are always the choosers, not the chosen.

When she finally does fall in love, where for the first time in her life her heart impels her to behavior her intellect recognizes as absurd, the man she loves rejects her. When she presses him for a reason, he succumbs to her importuning and blurts out the truth: she *bores* him. This revelation is the most insupportable blow yet to her self-esteem. When she rallies and falls in love once more—the greatest love of her life—she is thwarted again. This time it is by her lover's selfish children. She has met a man at last who fully reciprocates her feelings, but he is much older than she (in his 50s—she is in her 30s) and his children break up the affair. Fanny believes that they are afraid he will leave her money when he dies, and so for the sake of a few dollars they sacrifice his hopes of peace and love in his late years. An ugly world.

In the Epilogue, the editor meets her again and they have a long discussion about some of the issues raised in the story. During this talk the editor gets a less sympathetic impression of her than he had received through the tale. Her reiterated claim to being merely an ignorant, humble and uneducated woman he perceives as a cloak for her narrowness and self-righteousness. She

now looks to him "as hard as an old bagel." Despite her claim
to an interest in socialist ideas, he finds her obsessed with one
subject only: love and marriage, and the relations between men
and women. She displays an uneasy mixture of extraordinary
knowledge—in her subject she reads everything she can get her
hands on—and the coarsest ignorance. The editor lectures her at
length, simply and clearly, but she never really accepts what he
says. She does not seem to understand the implications of the
socialist solution to society's problems, including family relations and aspects of the woman question. He explains that morality is always relative to the class or group in power, so that if
she was puzzled at the double standard, she should see it as
made by and benefiting men, who had the power to impose
their morality because they were the breadwinners in family relations. When women were equal, they would share in creating
a new, more equitable morality. Of course, socialism did not
pretend to have answers for everything—it could no more relieve
the pain of unrequited love than it could that of a toothache.
The editor continues with disquisitions on the history of the
rise of a money economy, the inevitable combination of workers in the era of industrial production as the instruments for the
overthrow of capitalism, and other Marxist ideas, but anything
not bearing directly upon her obsession glances off her consciousness. Basically, she refuses to be broadened. Her portrait,
and that of the didactic editor, are lightened somewhat in the
last line of the novella, when she asks, all too humanly, " 'When
were you planning to publish my piece?' " She is a writer after
all.

The work is written in Cahan's usual plain Yiddish, and is
full of familiar Jewish types drawn from his vast experience. On
the whole it seems unnecessarily drawn out and, except for dis-
cussions on the power of sex, not as subtle as some of his earlier
English efforts. Fanny is interesting as a case study, and her un-
conscious self-revelation is nicely presented, but the reader may
find himself too close to the view taken by one of her lovers
and the editor: boredom and irritation. That Cahan thought the
book good enough for Yiddish publication as late as 1913, but

never for English publication, reveals again the somewhat lower status he afforded Yiddish as a literary vehicle—at least in his own work.

One measure of the lack of literary sophistication Cahan assumed in his Yiddish audience may be his attitude towards narrative point-of-view. "Fanny's Khasonim" appeared in the same year he was publishing "The Autobiography of an American Jew" in *McClure's Magazine,* his most extensive attempt to write a fiction wholly in the first person. In the Yiddish story, the first-person technique is attempted only within a protective Prologue and Epilogue—assurance, almost, to the reader that the worthy editor was different from and wiser than the narrator. No such assurance, apparently, would be offered to the reader of "The Autobiography of an American Jew" or *The Rise of David Levinsky,* the complex novel that was to grow from the *McClure's* story.

But "Fanny's Khasonim" cannot be dismissed, whatever its faults. The focus on the woman question and on the socialist attitudes suggested as the answer to it is intelligently double-edged, sophisticated. There is a dramatically effective opposition set up between the editor and Fanny. Hers is a good persona, since a more rigorously intellectual woman might not have been as accessible to the average reader. Self-taught, dogmatic, slightly ridiculous, Fanny is nevertheless very present and alive in the story. Cahan's—or the editor's—wrestling with this intractable woman brings the issues into bold relief.

What is salutary about Cahan's treatment of woman in all of his work generally is the absence of the stereotypic Yiddishe Mamma. There are no sentimentalized, heroic kinds like Michael Gold's mother in *Jews Without Money,* nor the nagging, cloying types like Sophie Portnoy in *Portnoy's Complaint.* Cahan's women are by and large individualized; most of them *do* things, have separate and recognizable consciousnesses, and strengths outside the traditional wife-mother roles. Of the three women we will see in David Levinsky's life, two are intellectuals, while only one chooses the traditional role. Even she displays a strength of personality larger than the role she chooses, and when she realizes at the end that the daughter for whom she makes the choice is unworthy, she bears her disappointment when she realizes at the end that the daughter for whom she makes the choice is unworthy, she bears her disappointment with pride and dignity.

Many of the women in Cahan's stories may indeed marry or, like Fanny, want to, but they do not lose themselves in the role. Tanya in "Circumstances" remains a pure intellectual, Sophie Leib is enigmatic still, Flora may be an allrightnik, but her ambition raises her above the girls of her set, Clara Yavner in *The White Terror and the Red* remains impossibly idealistic. Whatever one may say of any of them, there is not an earth-mother among them. Even in *Yekl,* the traditional Gitl starts as child-and-kitchen centered, but soon learns the limitations of that world and ends by dreaming of the grocery store she will own with Bernstein. Cahan the socialist seems more aware of the realities and potentialities of women's lives than are provided in more sentimental versions of Jewish women locked happily into traditional roles. His women toil, think, hold firm to ideals, or have none; act well or badly, suffer, and communicate independent spirits. As the didactic Yiddish editor he may lecture (perhaps ineffectually) the exasperating Fanny; but this unenlightened woman communicates a stubborn and even admirable sense of self when she speaks in her own voice. On his literary side, which is most often English, and not explicitly socialist, Cahan tends to allow that voice.

CHAPTER EIGHT

The White Terror and the Red:
Jewish Experience vs. Revolutionary Ideology

Cahan was of course conscious of his position as a bridge between disparate worlds of experience. Among the Yankees a
Jew, among Jews an expert on the American scene; in capitalist
America a radical socialist, among radicals a moderate; an intellectual and popularizer; a Russian soul and education jostling
alongside a Jewish and American one. And the persistent pull in
him, presumably resolved by his editorship of the *Forward*, of a
Jewish and Socialist identity. He never was able to complete
The Chasm, a novel he then contemplated which was supposed
to explore all the dichotomies of culture within himself and so
many of his immigrant generation. Instead of that proposed major work, two years after his return to the *Forward* Cahan published *The White Terror and the Red: A Tale of Revolutionary
Russia*—an ambitious novel of forty-two chapters and well over
four hundred pages, that deals largely with the problem of rec-
onciling a consciousness of Jewishness with the demands of the
revolutionary spirit.

The White Terror and the Red draws on Cahan's knowledge
of Russia's revolutionary and conspiratorial history, centering
upon the 1881 assassination of Czar Alexander II and its aftermath. In a way, it is Cahan's act of homage to his past. It honors
the Russian martyrs who kept alive the selfless spirit of the rev-

olution; it is also sharply critical of the anti-Semitism that dis-figured that spirit. Cahan exposes the reactionary forces that manipulate and profit from this insidious malady. The imagina-tive return to the year 1881 is of great significance to him: in Sanders' splendid observation, it was "the year Cahan entered as a Russian revolutionary and departed from as a Jew once again and for all time."[1]

These questions had become acute once more for Cahan in the year 1903 with the Kishinev massacres and the expulsion of the *Yiddishe Arbeiter Bund* (a Socialist organization for Jew-ish workers in Russia and Poland) from the Russian Social Dem-ocratic Federation (upon the initiative of Lenin and Trotsky). Like all Jews, Cahan was shaken by the massacres in Russia; he was quick to understand, as well, their political and social signif-icance. In an article in the *North American Review,* he exposed the origin of the Kishinev pogrom in a "blood libel" invented by the Czarist secret police, and explained that the purpose was to turn the masses against the Jews and away from any revolu-tionary activities.[2] The process he had seen at work in 1881 was being grimly repeated.

That there was such a reservoir of anti-Semitism among the masses that could be whipped up, and that Jews had perforce to be conscious of and respond to it, seemed clear enough to Ca-han and others. Yet there were revolutionaries who ignored the reality of a Jewish identity or even opposed specifically *Jewish* measures of resistance. The expulsion of the Bund, with which Cahan and the *Forward* had close ties, showed that the domi-nant revolutionary current refused to accommodate such a "particularist" and "nationalist" position. Cahan had seen that attitude at work before, when he had failed to get the Interna-tional Socialist Congress to denounce the anti-Semitism of the Dreyfus affair. With a sense that history was repeating itself, he sought to deal with these questions in *The White Terror and the Red.* When the book appeared in February 1905, the first Rus-sian Revolution had taken place, which made the work extreme-ly timely; unfortunately, a wave of pogroms in various cities within a few months blunted the revolutionary impetus in ways precisely and prophetically depicted in the novel.

A Long and Tendentious Novel

The White Terror and the Red centers on Prince Pavel Boulatoff's and Clara Yavner's involvement with the underground
revolutionary movement, and with each other, in Russia between 1874 and 1881. Cahan enriches the story with portraits
of other revolutionaries and their clandestine activities and of
the socially different worlds of the two lovers—one a nobleman
and Gentile, the other a commoner and Jew. It is his most tendentious work in English. Unfortunately it has long been out of
print so that a rather full summary is necessary.

In the first five chapters we are shown Pavel's development
from a conservative Czarist to membership in the revolutionary
movement. A student demonstration in his home town of Miroslav stimulates him to learn more about the reform movement,
and when he gets to St. Petersburg he makes contact with the
underground (through a former Talmud student named Makar).
Five years pass, during which the "going to the people" phase
of the movement has failed and induced them to become secret
and terroristic. Pavel is now a member of the Executive Committee.

After a failed plot upon the life of the Czar, Makar returns to
Miroslav with a plan to be arrested and then effect an escape
that will sow confusion in the ranks of the police. Pavel doesn't
think much of the plan but follows Makar to Miroslav. His mother discovers that he is one of the terrible Nihilists she has read
about (in Turgenev), but her horror is quickly dispelled when
she reads his literature and approves of the group's aims. Pavel
is lionized by the local revolutionaries, and at the home of Orlovsky, a government clerk and underground leader, he finally
meets Clara Yavner, the girl whose leading role in the demonstration five years earlier had launched Pavel on his new life.
They meet frequently to make plans—at her home in the Jewish
section, where he is not likely to be recognized—go for long
walks, eat wild strawberries, fall in love. He tells his mother,
who is not entirely pleased, but makes no effort to prevent the
liaison; on her part, Clara finds it impossible to tell her orthodox parents about Pavel, despite her liberation from any religious or national loyalties.

Clara's Jewishness has nevertheless been much in evidence and is frequently useful to her in revolutionary work. She also engages in spirited debates with her cousin Vigdaroff, an assimilationist Jew whose great passion is Russian literature and culture. She believes his views are illusory. She remains loyal to her parents, their tongue and basic values—eventually a source of much conflict for her.

In the process of Makar's escape, Clara's cover is revealed and she must become "ne-legalny"—an illegal person, without valid papers, hunted by the police. Back in St. Petersburg with Pavel, she meets other notorious ne-legalnys, such as Sophia, daughter of a former governor of St. Petersburg, and Hessia Helfman. Clara closely identifies with Hessia, who is also a Jewish revolutionist, and is married to a Gentile and nobleman. Pavel desperately pleads for Clara to marry him immediately so that they may gain such happiness as they can. But the capture of the most careful conspirator in their circle confirms her belief that they will all be ultimately apprehended; the best policy, she believes, remains self-abnegating dedication to the cause, not the illusion of personal happiness.

Finally, a plot to kill the Czar succeeds. Four men and a woman trap the Czar's vehicle on a local bridge; two bombs are thrown, the second fatally. The first bomber gives names to the police and a series of arrests follow. Six regicides in all are taken, tried, and sentenced to be executed. Among them are Sophia, the first woman to be executed in Russia since 1719, and Hessia, whose sentence is commuted to life imprisonment because she is pregnant. She and her baby soon die in prison, however, because of maltreatment. The deaths profoundly affect Clara, who will never forget her comrades' sacrifice in the cause of their great revolutionary ideals.

Anti-Jewish riots erupt in various cities, encouraged by the new Czar, who sees in them a diversion for the restless people and a way to assert Russian national unity. The Nihilists do not see the riots as another phase of the white terror but rather as an example of the ability of the Russian masses to move in a revolutionary fashion. They theorize that if the people can attack Jewish usurers, they can be led to recognize and attack the other enemies of the people in the regime itself. They overlook the fact that the few usurers among the Jews go relatively untouched, while the great mass of Jews, especially the numerous poor, suffer most. This situation impels several Jews in the radical movement, Elkin—a Miroslav leader—among them, to rethink their position and assert their Jewish identity. Others, like Vladimir and Dr. Lipnitzky, an assimilated Army doctor, recognize that the hope of assimilation is deluded, and they, too, assert their Jewish identity. Vladimir is even drawn into a militant Jewish defense group of workers and artisans. Clara is in deep conflict, as is, ultimately, Pavel. He had at first echoed the Nihilist line uncritically, but his instinctive sense of justice is aroused in the course of a vicious pogrom that overtakes Miroslav. After much soul-searching, Clara remains in the movement. A month after the riot in Miroslav, she and Pavel marry in Moscow.

Less than a month later, Pavel, too, has become illegal. Clara is still in turmoil over the Jewish question, but the image of the martyred Sophia and Hessia keep her dedicated to the revolutionary cause. She determines to go to Miroslav again, in the face of all danger, in order to persuade Elkin and others not to abandon the revolution. In Miroslav, Elkin tells her he is going to America (as is her cousin Vladimir). Clara feels he is leaving the cause for good, but his plan is to start Jewish Communist societies there, raise money, and otherwise support the revolution from that base. Clara's companion Olga is recognized by a spy, and arrested. Orlovsky prevails upon Elkin, on the eve of his departure for America, to go to Moscow to inform Pavel of her arrest. A few days later, Orlovsky and other members of the Miroslav circle are arrested, Makar has fallen into a trap, Pavel and Elkin are taken in a Moscow café. Within months, all are imprisoned, presumably until death, in solitary confinement in Trubetzkoy Bastion. Messages are tapped laboriously through walls, between Makar, Pavel, Elkin (who forgives Pavel, and does not regret being where he is rather than in America). Clara arrives in the prison, but is placed in a section far removed from her husband. A message of love finally comes through walls, floors, ceilings, to Pavel, who ends the book with his face buried in his hands, an image of great despair.

The Novel's Uniqueness and Distinction

The literary space occupied by this ambitious novel may be assessed in two ways: against the standard of the popular and successful novels of its day—and it did achieve a respectable success—one may claim for it outstanding qualities; in a larger literary context, which would include works by Henry James and Joseph Conrad, who each wrote notable novels concerned as this one is with terrorist politics, Cahan's achievement may not seem to be of the highest order.

There is no question that measured against Graustarkian melodrama or Francis Marion Crawford's historical romances—the general pattern of escape and fantasy characteristic of most American popular novelists' treatment of foreign lands and politics—Cahan's tale of revolutionary Russia stands out. The author is serious, he intends to inform truly, and he brings to the task practically first-hand knowledge of events and characters. Almost all of his contemporary critics praised his realistic portrayal of revolutionary Russia.

Cahan brings us to the heart of the action. We see how explosives are prepared and transported by the underground, the mechanics of illegal organization, the route of the Czar and the preparations made by his executioners on the day of his assassination. The characterization of political types and the dynamics of political meetings ring true. The portrayal of Russians on various social levels, drawn from Cahan's reading as well as his experience, display him at his shrewd best. And, as usual, the scenes of Jewish life and the knowledge of Jewish history, customs, ethos are many-sided, informed and informative.

More significantly, the novel is ideologically sophisticated. Especially good are the scenes touching issues close to Cahan—those in which the conflict between experience and ideology sharpens in the Jewish comrades. When the revolutionary movement sanctions anti-Semitic riots as a form of incipient class--

awakening among the Russian peasants ("the Socialism of
fools," in Bebel's great phrase), Vigdaroff, Clara, Elkin and all
the other Jews are confronted with existentially significant moments. Everything must be rethought. In the course of their debates, Cahan shows the variety and importance of the responses
in the Jewish world. Finally, for all his sympathy for the Nihilists' courage and idealism, the novel is a serious critique of their
methods and philosophy. The hard realities of the Jewish question—for which there is no solution within the given revolutionary assumptions—come to dominate the book.

In sum, Cahan's achievement in the novel is that he brings to
it the special perspective of one who had been a participant in
the movement that led to 1881 and who is still a radical. His
story depends upon a radical consciousness of the roots of the
Czarist despotism and of the revolutionary response to it, and
upon a Realist's concern for the facts. That concern does not
permit him to overlook the peculiarly bitter problems of the
Jewish revolutionaries—so important a part of that history. His
concerns and consciousness certainly distinguish him from the
popular writers of his day and assure a place for *The White Terror and the Red* among important documents of the time.

When all of this is said and done, I am not sure the novel will
kindle the imagination of the contemporary reader. One flaw
from a contemporary perspective is the unrelenting idealism
with which he endows Pavel Boulatoff and Clara Yavner. Cahan's usual realism and his admiration for frankness in dealing
with the relations between men and women desert him when
he deals with his two central characters. One appreciates from
documents the great spirituality, the almost incandescent idealism, that often characterized early Russian revolutionaries. As
if aware of this, and in the grip of his own nostalgia for a somewhat idealized past (Cahan's connection with the revolutionary
movement was, after all, not so great), he envelops the affair
between Pavel and Clara in a romantic glow. Their relationship is
unrelentingly moral, frequently sentimentalized in expression,
almost never physical. The ending, with the message of love
transmitted (with what endless tapping!) by all the noble comrades in prison, is pure bathos.

Other failures are imaginative. Characters like Pavel's mother and Makar's father figure brightly for a short space, convert to the revolutionary cause with unbelievable rapidity, and then are dropped from any significant connection with the novel. The behavior of Elkin—who has been so intelligent at gauging the importance to Jewish revolutionaries of the anti-Semitic riots— professing happiness in prison at the end (instead of going to America) defies credibility. Makar's plan for confusing the police is childish and as the chief vehicle for bringing together various strands of plot and character it makes the whole structure of the book seem implausible. Overall, the two worlds of historical fact—often presented in great essayistic chunks by Cahan —and imaginative truth (even when one can allow it credibility) tend to exist side by side, not fully assimilated to the total pattern of the novel.

To aid in a final assessment of the book's achievements and failures, it will be instructive to return for a moment to the books about terrorism by Conrad and James mentioned earlier.

Conrad's *The Secret Agent,* James's *The Princess Casamassima,* seem to me superior imagined worlds to Cahan's creation, yet Cahan's very failure can alert us to a fresh perception of it and of these highly esteemed works. Chiefly, we should see that Conrad's terrorists and agents, in their warped sickness, are even more tendentiously conceived than Cahan's idealized bomb-throwers. If the motives in *The White Terror and the Red* are impossibly pure, the motives in *The Secret Agent* (published two years later than Cahan's book) are impossibly corrupt. Conrad's own conspiratorial experience (on the right) like Cahan's (on the left) was brought to play in his novel, one for the purpose of condemnation, the other for celebration. The contemporary sensibility may prefer Conrad's complicated sense of evil —in which the destruction of innocence delivers nothing, points to no redemption, only blank moral horror—to Cahan's depiction of an innocence sacrificed in the present for a future redemption by history. That is a matter of taste and historical perspective. James attempts to transcend these categories. The world of his novel is ultimately less purely political than either of the others. At the end of *The Princess Casamassima* the sacrifice of the innocent lamb is a self-abnegating triumph complete unto itself.

Despite its failures, for all the fantasy involved in the love relationship or the self-sacrificing quality of the revolutionists that mars Cahan's novel, it remains a serious effort to inform us truly about a world rooted in historical reality—and in that respect it may still be a more useful book than either Conrad's or James'.

CHAPTER NINE

Getting It All Together:
The Rise of David Levinsky

For many years it was as if *The White Terror and the Red* marked the end of Cahan's aspirations towards a literary career in English. He emerged from that book's investigation of 1881 as, once again and unequivocally, a Jewish intellectual. Between 1905 and 1913 he enjoyed great success and extraordinary influence in the Jewish community. Those were the years of the largest Jewish immigration, during which Cahan was an arbiter in labor disputes, a political force, literary guide and mentor of the masses and the intelligentsia. The "worthy editor" of the powerful *Forward* was asked to play many roles—rabbi, historian, psychiatrist—and, indeed, Cahan performed them all with zest.

Worthy Mr. Editor,

I am a young woman, married eight years to a man who came from Russia, and we have four beautiful children. My husband's parents were killed in a pogrom and he alone barely escaped with his life. Later he was forced to leave Russia and he came to America.

Since the world-famous case of Mendel Beilis began in Russia, my husband doesn't miss reading anything that is written about it. And every time he finishes reading something in the newspaper about the bloodthirsty trial he gets so upset, so nervous, that he sometimes shows signs of madness. More than once I've been afraid to stay alone in the house with him.

At first it was bearable, but lately the news about the trial affected his nerves so much that he took it into his head that he must go back to Russia to take revenge on Beilis's persecutors. He had already packed his bags, but when he began to take leave of the children, to say good-by, they began to cry so bitterly that he remained at home. But he keeps on saying that he must go to Russia to take revenge on those who falsely accused Beilis of the ritual murder and on the pogromists who killed his own parents.

A few days ago he went to a lawyer and signed over to me and the children the few hundred dollars he has in the bank. He told them he did this so that, in case something happened to him in Russia, the children and I would at least have a few dollars.

Therefore, dear Editor, I need your advice. Maybe your answer will calm him a little, and he will put these ideas out of his head.

I thank you in advance,
Mary

Answer: Thousands of Jews came to America with their pogrom wounds that still bleed and can never be completely healed. And is it any wonder that this writer's husband has shattered his nerves? The murderers there killed his parents, almost brought about his death, and now the dreadful Beilis trial has reopened his old wounds.

Russia is full of such people, Jews and non-Jews, who feel the same hatred as he for the "Black Hundreds," and if it were possible to take revenge on the guilty ones they wouldn't wait for him to come all the way from America. But time will pay them what's due them. This man must calm himself, he must have pity on his wife and children and stop thinking of leaving them. The most important point is, however, the wife must take him to a good psychiatrist.[1]

Cahan was in many respects a fulfilled man—but the old literary dream died hard. In 1913 he undertook a writing assignment that brought him back once more to the problem of composing imaginative literature for a general American public. It was to lead to the work by which he is best known. In that year he published a series in *McClure's Magazine* called "The Autobiography of an American Jew" that became the basis for *The Rise of David Levinsky* a few years later.

The visibly large number of Jews now in New York and the prominence of some of them prompted the editor of *McClure's* to ask Cahan for two articles on the subject of Jewish immigrant successes in American business. The request had in it something less than innocent, since *McClure's* was the leading muck-raking journal at the time. One would imagine that articles on that subject might expose Jews to an anti-Semitic backlash, so that Cahan's acceptance of the assignment had some element of risk in it. Cahan, the leading interpreter of Jews to the American world, took on the assignment, and transformed it.

In the first place, his contributions were not "articles" at all. His most telling decision about the subject was to cast the story of Jewish business success in America as a first person narrative —in the voice and with the sensibility of a rich garment manufacturer. It was a story Cahan knew well and which he humanized, complicated, avoided stereotyping. It also unlocked deep resources in himself, despite the fact that the central persona was a successful capitalist, the very antithesis of the intellectual and socialist Cahan. The pieces turned out so well the editor asked for two more.

Many elements in the life and sensibility of the central character (whom he called David Levinsky) related to the author in a subtle personal way as well as in the broad areas of experience common to many Jewish immigrants. Cahan had devised a strategy for combining subjective and objective aspects of the material, for presenting a personal story as well as the saga of a people, and for holding in balance criticism and celebration. It was a balancing act for which he had practiced most of a lifetime. Expanded and enriched, the series became *The Rise of*

David Levinsky in 1917. That book, as John Higham perceptively notes, combines the distinctly American theme of success with a Jewish subject matter and a Russian artistic sensibility.[2] Into it Cahan put all of his rich experience, all he had learned about life and writing. In my view it is a major American work, indebted to but transcending Howells' *The Rise of Silas Lapham,* and with a central character as significant and interesting as many of Dreiser's towering creations.[3]

The Novel Summarized

The general scheme of David Levinsky is relatively simple, despite its length and its division into fourteen "books" or sections. In 1913, presumably, at the age of fifty-two (Cahan's age at the time), the narrator—David Levinsky—looks back upon his life from the vantage point of his success as a garment manufacturer "with more than two million dollars." In the first part of the book he recalls his past in the *shtetl* of Antomir in Russia, the death of his mother at the hands of Gentiles, his days as an impoverished Talmud student. When he emigrates to the United States in 1885 (with money given him by a young woman) he arrives, as he says, "with four cents in my pocket." Thereafter, for four-fifths of the book the scene is America and the story chronicles Levinsky's rise from peddler to rich man. In the process much of the social history of Jewish immigrant life is made vivid: the teeming East Side streets, sweatshops, factories, union activities, the growth of the great New York garment industry. We move from factory lofts and offices to real-estate speculations on the "curb" in Harlem. We get inside the Catskill resorts of the *nouveau riche,* and the apartments of designers, business tycoons and intellectuals. Cultural changes and conflicts are depicted through the struggle for mastery of language, the relations of "Americanized" children with immigrant parents, awareness of such new emotional possibilities as "love." Above all, there is an acute sensitivity to the effects of these elements of growth, change, conflict upon the character and inner life of the narrator. Levinsky is a reflective type, an intellectual of sorts, who attempts to articulate the meaning of his experiences.

"Am I happy?" he asks in the final chapter—and concludes, "My sense of triumph is coupled with a brooding sense of emptiness and insignificance, of my lack of anything like a great, deep interest. . . . No, I am not happy." It is, finally, a complex book whose central themes are more elusive than the surface suggests. The "rise" of David Levinsky presents problems that have been compared with Silas Lapham's and Carrie Meeber's (*Sister Carrie*), but which differ from theirs in significant ways. Even in this brief résumé Cahan's recapitulation of some of the major themes in his life's work can be seen.

In the first four books, "Home and School," "Enter Satan," "I Lose My Mother," and "Matilda," David Levinsky tells of his growing up in and finally leaving Antomir, a town in Russia. His father died when David was less than three years old, and he is brought up in direst poverty by his mother. They live in a corner of a basement room shared with three other families in the poorest section of town. His mother is devoted to him and determined that he shall receive religious instruction despite their poverty. David is a good student, but the erratic and sometimes missing payments for his teachers frequently result in his being singled out for beatings.

He and his mother are tenacious, however, and he is ultimately admitted to a free Talmudic seminary, where it is customary for the students to sleep on benches in the study hall, and to receive meals donated by orthodox households in the community. He is befriended by an older man and Talmud scholar, Reb Sender, and a young fellow student, Naphtali. After graduation, at sixteen, David continues his studies as an "independent scholar" at the Preacher's Synagogue. Despite the exhortations of Reb Sender and cautionary tales from the Talmud, he is bedeviled by thoughts of women. He betrays other unscholarly traits: at one point his passion for study is fueled by hatred for a rival scholar whom he wants to surpass with feats of learning.

His mother's joy in him as a scholar is short-lived. Always ready to rush to his defense, she runs out into the market-place one day in order to attack some Gentiles who have struck and mocked David. She is brought back with her head broken, and she dies. After the initial sympathy and aid he receives as an orphan, David's poverty deepens and he literally never has enough to eat. He often goes without food as he sways over his Talmud volumes.

To David's great surprise and anger, his friend Naphtali reveals that he no longer believes in God. But then David quickly accommodates to this new revelation. Naphtali introduces him to books of science, poetry, fiction, religious criticism, all of which David enjoys, although they do not deeply interest him. Naphtali induces Shiphrah Minsker, a rich woman given to sudden excesses of piety, to provide meals for David. With enough to eat, at last, Levinsky finds he does not return diligently to Talmud studies. Instead he is hungry for change and sensation—and at that point his fancy is caught by the possibility of immigration to America, a current idea among Jews as a consequence of of the anti-Semitic riots after 1881.

For Levinsky, it is chiefly the mystery of the place that lures him. Reb Sender is appalled at David's plan to go to America— for him a place in which "one becomes a Gentile." After a sickness, David is taken by the charitable Shiphrah Minsker to live in her house, where he meets her "modern," educated, and attractive daughter, Matilda. Matilda at first thinks him only amusing, but soon takes an interest in him. She urges him to cast off his old fashioned ways and to get a real education. David falls in love with her. She allows many embraces and kisses —and would probably "go all the way," but David, much to her disgust, fails to understand her cues. She gets the money for him to go to America, which he accepts with mixed feelings. He believes he will not be able to live without her. She is out of patience with him, however, encourages him to go, and he does.

The next four books, "I Discover America," "A Greenhorn No Longer," "My Temple," and "The Destruction of My Temple" tell of his first days in America—his fall from piety and chastity, his early efforts to learn English, his educational aspirations, his beginnings at work and in the business world.

His first day in America he wanders its streets in a whirl. After some initial disappointments, he is helped by a wealthy synagogue member, who outfits him in new clothes and gives him some money. With this, Levinsky acquires his first lodgings and a small amount of goods to peddle. He is acutely homesick. Levinsky soon falls from piety, as all around him predict, and he shaves his beard. He becomes "a greenhorn no longer" in other ways as well, when he flirts with his first two landladies and finally loses his chastity with women of the streets. He now realizes why Matilda found him so naive—a discovery that only further endears her memory to him.

His education and Americanization proceed apace. From a prostitute—a former resident of Antomir—he receives instruction in the realities of American politics. She informs him about "bosses," political parties, district leaders, "favors." This knowledge—and what he sees for himself on his first Election Day— conflicts with the idealized version of politics he hears at the public evening school he has enrolled in. At school, his language teacher, Mr. Bender, befriends him because of his enthusiasm and aptness for learning. Upon "graduation," Bender gives him a copy of *Dombey and Son.* Levinsky is soon deep in Dickens and Thackeray—and begins to neglect his meager peddling business. His hardest time in America follows—flophouses, cadging change from acquaintances. At this low point he meets Gitelson, a tailor he had not seen since they were shipboard companions. Gitelson is doing well and persuades Levinsky to learn a trade. He is apprenticed to a sewing machine operator and begins to earn wages that grow (along with his pride) as his skills increase. He dreams of saving money to attend City College—even proposing marriage to Gussie, a thrifty shop-mate, so that she might support him through school—a common enough practice among immigrants (she refuses). His interests expand. With a new friend, Jake Mendels, he begins attending the Jewish theater regularly. He meets the son of his new landlord—a wealthy businessman named Meyer Nodelman. Nodelman employs Levinsky briefly as his English tutor, but the venture soon ends and Levinsky must return to shopwork in order to save money for college.

An incident at work causes him great humiliation and is the occasion for his striking out on his own. He inadvertently spills milk on some goods, whereupon one of the bosses, Jeff Manheimer, calls him a "lobster." The insult festers, and Levinsky determines to go into business for himself if he can induce the Manheimers' designer, Ansel Chaikin, to go in with him. Using his charm and shrewdness (he has very little capital) he persuades Mrs. Chaikin to have faith in him and allow her husband to contribute his work. The venture operates on a shoestring; he is forced to go to all his acquaintances for credit or help at one time or another. After receiving credit from a consignment merchant he is able to fill an order from the midwest that he had won with much ingenuity. The western firm fails and the check which was to deliver him from his debtors does not arrive. It is the temporary end of the business—but the permanent end of his college aspirations. Despite the loss he is now determined to continue somehow as a manufacturer.

Book IX, "Dora," is the longest in the novel and is chiefly about his second love affair, although it is artfully interspersed with his growing business affairs. Meyer Nodelman helps him with a loan at his great moment of need. While he is desperately searching for other lenders, the check does arrive from the restored midwest firm and he is back in business. Max Margolis, a friend of his peddling days, is sympathetic to Levinsky and invites him into his home. He meets Max's wife Dora and their daughter Lucy, and develops a warm friendship with all of them. Filling business orders happily, he is nevertheless lonely and seeks out Max for advice about his affairs—chiefly to have the consoling presence of the family. He becomes a regular visitor at the Margolises and at last a boarder there. Dora and he exchange confidences; a relationship between them grows. She tells of her feelings as her child learns to read—a mixture of jealousy and pride. Wanting her child to respect her, she too learns to read and "Americanize" her manners. Levinsky tells her of his love affair with Matilda. Dora is intrigued—her own marriage having been an arranged one, not based on love. Intimate talks between them continue for weeks. He tells her, finally, that he loves her. She reveals that she loves him, but forbids further talk about themselves. She finally gives in to her powerful feelings—her first experience of "love"—and dotes upon Levinsky's presence in her life. They do not, however, consummate the affair.

Meanwhile, Levinsky is prospering in business. For a while the
the nascent Cloak Makers Union threatens his shop, because orthodox Jews are willing to work there for less than union wages
in order to observe their Sabbath. The Socialist press calls him
"a cockroach manufacturer" (which annoys him) and "a fleecer
of labor" (which pleases him, since it puts him in the company
of Vanderbilt, Gould, Rothschild). He continues his clandestine
relations with the orthodox, non-union workers, which gives
him a great competitive advantage when other manufacturers
lock out the union. He has begun to read Darwin and Spencer
and conceives of himself now as among the fittest, and of failures as misfits.

The affair with Dora reaches a climax. Thinking she is about
to lose him, she abandons herself to him and they consummate
the affair. He is ecstatic, but the next day she is full of remorse.
He wants her to divorce Max and start over with him. She refuses and he has to leave the household—much to Max's bewil-
derment.

The title of Book X, "On the Road," refers to selling "on the
road"—Levinsky as a "drummer," a traveling salesman. For him
it is "a great school of business and life." Chaikin having withdrawn from their partnership, Levinsky hires his former teacher
Bender as a bookkeeper, which frees him for the road. He closes
a very big deal in St. Louis that brings him national attention.
All of his business affairs thrive. During the prosperity following
the panic of 1893 he moves his shop to fine quarters on Broad-
way. He is more than ever confirmed in his social Darwinism.
Chaikin wants to be a partner again (he later returns to work
for Levinsky as a designer), Max Margolis wants to be friends
(Levinsky lies to him about the nature of his relationship to
Dora), a hated rival from the road days comes to work for him
as a salesman. Everything confirms his having "got there" (made
it). Except that he is still unmarried. The next three books,
"Matrimony," "Miss Tevkin," and "At Her Father's House,"
tell of his almost marrying one woman whom he does not love
and of his unsuccessful pursuit of another whom he does love.

Meyer Nodelman (who remains among his closest friends)
and others try to interest him in various women, but to no avail.

Levinsky finally decides in his fortieth year to marry Fanny
Kaplan, daughter of a wealthy businessman and Talmud scholar.
He is not in love with her, but the ambience of orthodoxy in her
father's house is pleasing to him, despite his atheism. A few
years earlier he had learned with much excitement that Matilda
was in New York, scheduled to appear at the Cooper Union
with her husband and another Russian refugee, in behalf of imprisoned revolutionaries in Russia. But when Levinsky came to
the lecture hall to meet her, after one look at his rich attire
she spurned him as a class enemy. This incident hardened his
detestation of all radicals. The antithesis of free-thinking and
socialism that he found at the Kaplans' seemed to offer him a
peaceful haven.

Shortly before he is to marry Fanny, however, he accidental-
ly encounters Anna Tevkin at a Catskill mountain resort. She is
young, beautiful, intelligent; he is smitten with her. She shows
little or no interest in him. When he discovers that her father is
a former Hebrew poet whose love letters to his wife had aroused
his and Naphtali's fascination back in Antomir, Anna seems
more desirable than ever. He breaks off the engagement with
Fanny quickly and unceremoniously, in order to pursue Anna
through her father.

Tevkin is now a rather poor real estate broker, and the father
of a large family of—as David Levinsky sees them—interesting
sons and daughters. Each is a partisan of one or another -ism
fashionable among the Jewish intelligentsia—Literary Modernism, Zionism, Cultural Nationalism, varieties of socialism. Levinsky is accepted as a friend of the father's. Mr. Tevkin is flattered
that someone of Levinsky's renown in business circles should
take such an interest in him. Furthermore, Levinsky has taken
out Tevkin's three books in Hebrew from the Astor Library and
can discourse knowledgeably—and admiringly—about them. He
becomes a regular visitor at the Tevkin's household. He over-
comes his antipathy towards radicalism, even contributing to
the children's various causes. During this time a fever of real estate speculation strikes New York and Levinsky is drawn into
it by Tevkin, almost to the point of ruin. His recklessness seems
to grow along with his frustration about Anna. Dora reappears

briefly, a mature and dignified woman with whom he has a nostalgic meeting; but his heart is full of Anna. She has supplanted Matilda and Dora as the greatest love he has ever felt.

At last he determines to talk to her about it– after a traditional Passover seder led by Tevkin, who in his late years has become drawn increasingly to the traditional ways. Anna rebuffs Levinsky completely, shocked that he has presumed again to mention love to her. He is crushed.

The last book, "Episodes of a Lonely Life," is an epilogue to the foregoing events. Defeated by Anna, he renews his hatred of socialists, awakens to the acute danger to his financial situation caused by his real estate speculations. With the aid of business friends he recoups and enters a new phase of even greater riches as a monopolist. Many old acquaintances return: Matilda is encountered at a theater benefit, pleasantly this time (she has mellowed after years in America). In 1910 he invites Gitelson to dine at the Waldorf-Astoria to celebrate the twenty-fifth anniversary of their arrival in America (the dinner is a fiasco because of the great social distance between them). He meets Gussie again, whose devotion to the cause of her fellow workers shames him into settling a strike he had bitterly resisted. All serve to emphasize his sense of loneliness.

The final chapter of this last book begins with the question "Am I happy?" He is lonely and still unmarried. A final relationship is recounted—with a sympathetic Gentile—which cannot overcome the chasm of their different—as he terms it— "races." The last words of the book echo the sadness of the first words. At the beginning of his story he had said:

> "And yet when I take a look at my inner identity it impresses me as being precisely the same as it was thirty or forty years ago. My present station, power, the amount of wordly happiness at my command, and the rest of it, seem to be devoid of significance."

His last words are:

> "I can never forget the days of my misery. I cannot escape from my old self. My past and present do not comport well.

David, the poor lad swinging over a Talmud volume at the Preacher's Synagogue, seems to have more in common with my identity than David Levinsky, the well-known cloak manufacturer."

The key to Levinsky's character and the book's meaning lies in these last words. Although his voice, mode of narration, selection and arrangement of material, do raise certain questions about how they are to be understood, these words can be taken straight, weighed and appreciated in their full import.

The Character of David Levinsky

There is, first, the question of Levinsky's reliability as a narrator. On one level he is a perfect persona for a realistic novelist in the Russian tradition—perceptive and shrewd in his evaluation of character (which he prides himself on), even-handed in displaying the good and the bad in himself. He is honest, direct, truthful—confessing to aspects of his character not wholly to his credit: dissembling over his Talmud studies, sharp business practices, unfair labor practices, visits to prostitutes, exploiting his mother's death for sympathy and advantage. Yet this candor may be self-serving, for in every case one can excuse his derelictions as being only too human. The deeper truth which his candor skirts may be that there is something *inhuman* in Levinsky, or to be less extreme in statement, upon close examination Levinsky reveals an emotional deficiency that prevents him from being fully human as that term is commonly understood.

One truth about Levinsky is that he is a great egoist, basically indifferent to, or manipulative of, others. His acts of philanthropy or piety frequently have a naked self-interest behind them that is not always acknowledged (his support of the Sons of Antomir's Synagogue is fed by nostalgia, but it also secures him a supply of non-union labor). Or, once away from the sewing machine himself, he is a typical "boss"—indifferent to his workers' long hours and hard lot. Even his employment of former acquaintances seems motivated by a confirmation of his own rise and superiority, unexpressed, that it affords him. Yet these

are obvious and perhaps minor examples of his egoism. There is
a deeper, and not always conscious, level at which Levinsky de-
ceives himself about the degree of his self-absorption.

Considered in this light, his complaints about a life devoid of
significance may be seen as a self-serving lament. It takes the
curse of success off the "sad millionaire"—a sly maneuver that
allows him to have his cake and eat it, too. Levinsky treasures
his ability to feel the poignance of his situation—a successful
man, and yet a failure in things that matter, affairs of the heart
and the spirit. It is a dignified awareness—which once again demonstrates his superiority to those of his contemporaries—Max
Margolis, Mrs. Chaikin, and an old Bohemian musician—whose
condition Levinsky presents to us as pathetic but without dignity.

The egoism is seen most clearly in Levinsky's frustrated love
affairs—which are as much the subject of the book as is the
meaning of business success. In the first affair with Matilda he
is a callow youth, but the same preoccupation with his own
feelings about the relationship and his insensitivity to the other's full reality is as evident as it will be later with Dora and
Anna. He is not loath to trade on this love affair to expedite
his affair with Dora. In the affair with Dora it is clear, too, that
he values as much the sense of "being in love" as he does the
relationship itself. "Being in love" confirms for him his modernity (really his being in the world). Indeed, his very sense of
worth depended on the ability to have an emotional response.
During the relationship with Matilda he had said, "I am in love.
I am no mere Talmud student."

The reasons for his finding Matilda "enchanting" reveal another trait of Levinsky's: his admiration of things non-Jewish,
aspects of a more desirable and radiant Gentile world. This trait
is persistent and faintly disagreeable to a contemporary reader,
although of course his attitude is often ambivalent. One example of his ambivalence is his yearning for an American college
education at the same time that he retains a snobbish European
attitude towards its inferiority to European university training.
Another is his aping Gentile manners in business (dressing "like
a genteel American") while privately cherishing his own intellec-

tual superiority. What he is awed by in Matilda is her Russian and German education, "her Gentile name [which] had a charm for my ear," the way she had of saying "Mother!" instead of "Mamma!" In America he feels at one point that "people who were born to speak English were superior beings."

At one period of his life he even sought out prostitutes "who were real American" (an ambiguity, given his disdain for the profession, which Levinsky leaves unexplored). All of this, of course, points to fundamental problems of his conception of self, of his own identity. The sense of a past and present that "do not comport well" begins to loom larger. David Levinsky's words express his fear that his personality lacks a coherent center.

Levinsky is able to compensate for his fear by retreating into his wealth and imagined superiority. He acts grandly when he suggests that Dora leave Max for him, but when it would take but a word to Max to clear the way for their coming together, he rather mysteriously (almost absent-mindedly) declines to give the word. He scarcely sees the real Fanny Kaplan, and in Anna Tevkin he pursues a hopeless illusion. What he values, finally, seem to be relationships that exist in his mind. Nodelman says of him, "Too much in his head, don't you know. You think too much, Levinsky. That's what's the matter. First marry and do your thinking afterward." The advice about marrying first and thinking afterward is stupid, of course, and part of Cahan's effort to show the basis of Levinsky's real superiority to others of his class, but there is a sense in which Nodelman does characterize him correctly. Like other Cahan characters discussed previously, Levinsky is self-absorbed, full of nostalgic yearning and a sense of his own unfulfilled desires. But unlike Zalkin or Tzinchadzi, it is that very sense that confirms for Levinsky his own superior sensitivity. Cahan presents a very sophisticated portrait: his Levinsky retains a kind of autonomy by being self-centered, aloof, alone. Something in him is always withdrawn, in reserve, judging his own actions—and he is, after all, a powerful man. It is a superior and chilling portrait, from which Levinsky emerges more like a Dreiserian titan of industry than a bourgeois Nodelman.

Language and Emotion

In the realm of language, that instrument for making experience comprehensible, Levinsky masters "good English," proudly and after much effort. But it is not the vehicle, finally, for embracing the divergent and unsettling paradoxes of his life. If there is a sense of emotional aridity in Levinsky, Cahan's art enables us to see it in the very language he uses to tell his story.

When Levinsky attempts to describe the meaning to him of his loss of his mother, what emerges is a *report* of the loss rather than a dramatization or lyric evocation of the emotions involved.

> As I went to bed on the synagogue bench, however, instead of in my old bunk at what had been my home, the fact that my mother was dead and would never be alive again smote me with crushing violence. It was as though I had just discovered it. I shall never forget that terrible night.

The emotional impact of the passage is stifled by the language; indeed it is never released because of the language. The passage is "correct," but lifelessly stiff ("the fact that," "It was as though I had just. . . ."), literary in the worst sense of that word ("smote me with crushing violence," "That terrible night"), above all *described*, as if from the outside. We are told that he was "crushed," and that the night was memorably "terrible"; there is no dramatization of these emotions. The passage is incapable of transmitting a fully dramatized sense of loss—a loss that was great and traumatizing (although that is only to be inferred from Levinsky's career). It was a world irretrievably lost, unassimilable to the writer in a language newly mastered and a sensibility that lacks fullness and assured amplitude.

In writing about another central experience in his life, Levinsky again is unable to overcome a certain distance from its emotional reality. He *points* to the emotion, but his rendering of it is blurred. I am referring to the critical experience of arriving in the New World.

> The immigrant's arrival in his new home is like a second birth to him. . . . I conjure up the gorgeousness of the spectacle as it appeared to me on that clear June morning: the magnifi-

cent verdure of Staten Island, the tender blue of sea and sky, the dignified bustle of passing craft—above all, those floating, squatting, multitudinously windowed palaces which I subsequently learned to call ferries.

In this passage we perceive language that seems to come to the writer second-hand. It is high-sounding and scrupulously literary: "I conjure up," "magnificent verdure," "tender blue," "dignified bustle"—and diction that is painfully pretentious: if Levinsky has learned to call "multitudinously windowed palaces" ferries, he apparently has not learned to call "verdure" trees and grass, nor a "spectacle" anything but "gorgeous." Levinsky again characterizes himself in language: correct, intelligent, self-satisfied, somewhat lifeless.

He opens the passage by describing the immigrant's arrival as a second birth—as indeed it was—but bemused by those ferries, where is the pain and glory and wonder of birth? Levinsky is really preoccupied with the contrast between what he is now and that other "green" Levinsky who thought that ferries were palaces. The experience of rebirth is completely side-tracked. In this passage there is the same failure to communicate an essential experience as in the other cited, and even more significantly, a failure of the narrator to fix exactly what it was he was trying to communicate. It is a blurring of focus common to Levinsky, and no doubt to Cahan and others of the immigrant generation.

From his earliest days as a Talmud scholar, reading in the sing-song method of study without having to attend to the substance of the words themselves, thinking about other things—indeed, with the very separation of Talmud Studies from his real life—Levinsky always felt a dissociation between thought and experience and between emotional reality and language. To this central dislocation were added the traumas of being orphaned and the abrupt transition to a startlingly new life in America, leaping centuries of experience, subverting everything previously known or believed. Levinsky's recognition of the incompatibility of his past and present—the difficulty of ever meaningfully getting the diverse parts of his life all together— is a central illumination, no mere rhetorical flourish.

What troubles David Levinsky, then, is how to put the incredible elements of his life together in a way that makes emotional and intellectual sense. He gets things together as a capitalist—buying, selling, wheeling and dealing—but emotionally he fails and is a fragmented, partial person. Two of Cahan's fictional forerunners of Levinsky share these characteristics and throw some light on Levinsky's character. We remember how women loved by Aaron Zalkin and Tzinchadzi had an intuitive distrust or final uneasiness with each of them. Something in Zalkin's looks turned Sophie off, Zelaya thought Tzinchadzi had no heart. Levinsky's bad luck with women parallels theirs. It is the result, perhaps of some final inability in Levinsky fully to know, and to give, what he was.

All that makes his fate seem unique and intensely personal. Of course it is, as all lives and all credibly presented fictional lives are, but there is a way to look at his experience as representative of something much broader. Cut off from his past, his mother (tongue), his father (land), all old beliefs and value systems, how can a David Levinsky be expected to overcome a sense of deep dislocation and alienation, how can he fill such a void and emerge integrated and whole? Posing such questions, the book may be seen as dealing quintessentially with the immigrant experience; put that way it is also a quintessentially American book.

The American Significance of The Rise of David Levinsky

Clearly, Levinsky—and behind him Cahan—was fascinated by America ("an American day seemed far richer in substance than an Antomir year") and by those who from humble origins became successful, i.e., rich, in America. It is a national fascination and of course permeates our literature. Usually, in our serious writers, the fascination with the pursuit of success is coupled with an attempt to show the price such a pursuit exacts. Howells presented his business man on the rise with a moral dilemma that he could resolve only by remaining honest and being content to go back to the farm. Dreiser's Carrie, from one point of view the heroine of an archetypal rags-to-riches story, is morally untroubled, has no place to go forward to—she is neither happy nor unhappy. Cahan's immigrant differs from each of these. For one thing, Silas Lapham had a farm (and a family with him) to go back to—where the old values that presumably come from that life would sustain him. (This resolution of the problem by Howells seems to me to represent psychological and social non-sense, a day dream or fantasy, not a reality or feasible alternative for the great mass of people.) Like Lapham, Levinsky had a background of firm values that had to be abandoned in the market-place—but unlike Lapham, the immigrant knew there was no going back. And unlike Carrie, who also knew there was no going back, his baggage from the old life also included many internalized values and ideals. Because the old community and its values left its vestigial traces, the individualistic American version of success was bound to be an ambivalent value to Levinsky.

Crevecoeur talks about "the new man" who leaves "behind him all his ancient prejudices and manners" in order to receive "new ones from the new mode of life he has embraced." In achieving the language and customs of the new land, Levinsky gives up, chiefly, his mother-tongue and the older Jewish values. The "mother-tongue" is literally that: the language in which all his mother's endearments, warmth, concern and love are con-veyed to him (so that thereafter her voice, presence, love were alive in his heart, he says, "like the Flame Everlasting in a syn-agogue"). Chief among the ancient values of the tribe that he gives up is contempt for wealth and the rewards of this ephem-eral world ("only good deeds and holy learning have tangible worth. Beware of Satan, Davie," says Reb Sender, his genial father figure). Cahan was no filial pietist, but he was too percep-tive not to see in his character the feeling of inner loss in his new life and a total contradiction between his two lives. That is emphasized in Levinsky's first and last words.

His past and present did "not comport well"—what a persist-ent motif among American writers—in some sense almost all of them immigrants or descendants of immigrants, country boys and girls in the city, city boys and girls in the country, western-ers in the east, easterners in the west, all embracing the conflict of cultures within them and in the society. For Levinsky the reason for the power of the success ethic is well-laid in the portrayal of his early poverty and deprivation, a fatherless child living in a basement with three other families, being beaten by his Hebrew teacher because he was a charity scholar. The portrayal of *shtetl* life is authentic—no Edenic idyll. For the immigrant, the American dream of acceptance into mainstream society, the promise of meaningful work and material well-being was obviously desirable—and of course still is for the dispossessed inside and out of our society. Yet the dilemma persisted: how to make up for the acute and inescapable sense of loss: of the mother, of childhood, of innocence. Despite everything, one kind of Paradise was lost. The rite of passage from one state to another was so much more than symbolic: the ocean crossing, the cutting off from one culture and the emergence in a new one, was absolute, complete, traumatic—a second birth.

The new world this new Adam was born into showed many unlovely sides, but in a passage of almost Jamesian astuteness, Levinsky embraces his complex new fate: for "while human nature was thus growing smaller, the human world was growing larger, more complex, more heartless, *and more interesting* [italics mine]." Levinsky says "yes" to the Satan old Reb Sender at home had warned him about ("Beware of Satan, Davie. When he assails you, just say no, turn your heart to steel and say no."). Rich in the things of this world, he finds at last that he has purchased them at the expense of his inner spirit. At the end Levinsky yearns for more spiritually satisfying fare than business and the success ethic. He envies those of his brethren who have distinguished themselves in science, music, art, and he says that if he had it to do all over again, he would *not* think of a business career. At the heart of whatever is self-serving rationalization in that statement, we must discern a legitimate and despairing hope for an elusive center that would stabilize and legitimate his American life.

So ends *The Rise of David Levinsky*—a haunting, suggestive, and I think finally, prophetic book. Two generations from Levinsky, many thoughtful people in the Jewish community speak of a spiritual *malaise* that seems to be present in its more

or less affluent American existence. Certainly this awareness is
discernible in the work of serious American-Jewish writers when
they explore their own ambivalent experience in this new world.
In the Jewish renaissance, and later, many writers have felt free
to use the materials of their lives in America—as Jews—without
an awkward and crippling defensiveness or sentimentality; part
of their impulse has been to discover, name and win back an
important part of themselves. Cahan, of course, was there first
—and his explorations can only now, perhaps, be justly appreciated. In *Augie March* and *Herzog*, it is the early days with
Grandma Lausch and on Napoleon Street in Montreal that Saul
Bellow communicates with feeling. Alfred Kazin's growing up
in *Walker in the City* seems to be more compelling than his later
book, *Starting Out in the Thirties,* in which the bedazzled
young graduate of City College breaks out of his ghetto into a
wider world of letters. In that world we are treated to literary
gossip instead of profound experience. Paul Jacobs asks at a crucial point of his life, when he is thrown back upon himself, *Is
Curly Jewish?* and discovers that inside the tough thirties radical
there was a young Jewish boy all along. Philip Roth puts all
these themes together in *Portnoy's Complaint.* In F. Scott Fitz-
gerald's investigation of the American Dream, *The Great Gats-
by,* Nick Carraway learns, too, that our past hopes and present
realities do not comport well, and that we have to think
through who and what we are—as Americans. "So we beat on,"
he says, "boats against the current, borne back ceaselessly into
the past." David Levinsky and Abraham Cahan both made the
journey—as we do, too, in discovering them.

After *David Levinsky*, Cahan wrote no more imaginative literature. The culmination of years of inner searching and of the
accumulation of much knowledge of the world around him,
and the consummation of a technique adequate to render this
dialectical relationship, Cahan could go no further in this direction. In the 1920s and 1930s, Cahan forsook further purely literary work of his own, encouraging others instead. He wrote
almost always in Yiddish now: a study of the Moscow Art Theater, a book on Palestine, various political studies, his five-volume memoir, a biography of the actress Rashell. Past sixty, the
inner and private man, whose voice is the key to any imaginative
and creative work, yielded to the public one. The *Forward* itself
had become an epic, the book of life that he had hoped to record in his earlier days. There was no further need to assay
stories and imagined fictions. As Sanders perceptively observes,
Cahan's autobiography really ends after the fourth volume, not
the fifth (which is largely given over to editorial and journalistic
matters). The fourth volume, published in 1928, concludes with
an account of the great birthday celebration given for Cahan in
Carnegie Hall in 1910—after that, as Cahan was to sense implicitly in the 1920s, his autobiography and the *Forward* "had
become one and the same." Cahan's *Forward* was the most im

portant and successful foreign language newspaper ever to be produced in America, and played a great role in the acculturation of the Jewish immigrant population. Cahan made his mark as well as an early socialist and trade union organizer and was influential all his life in social-democratic and garment-union circles. Steeped in politics and journalism and a product of Russian, Jewish and American culture, Cahan occupies a unique place in our social and intellectual history as he mediated between these various worlds.

He pursued this role of mediator in his literary work. His novels and stories are pioneering explorations of the subject of the immigrant in American life, with all its attendant dislocations and search in life and language for coherent expression. He gives us a major Realist's portrait of the setting for this search and touches poignantly on the yearning and loneliness of those seeking emotional wholeness. Insofar as we are "a nation of immigrants," Cahan's is an important American statement. Finally, his linguistic and rhetorical strategies place him at the beginning of the amazing development in this century of an American Jewish literature. When Kafka said to a Jewish audience in Prague, "You know more Yiddish, ladies and gentlemen, than you think you do," he could have been addressing most contemporary American-Jewish writers. If a Yiddish sensibility does figure in their work, the earliest vehicle of its transmission is Abraham Cahan.

Preface

1. At this writing there is no full, authoritative biography of Cahan. The indispensable source for the life is Cahan's five-volume autobiography *Bleter fun Mein Leben* (New York, 1926–1931). The first two volumes have been translated into English as *The Education of Abraham Cahan*, introd. Leon Stein (Philadelphia, 1969). These works hereafter cited as *Bleter* and *Education* in the text. Two works which rely heavily on the autobiography are Theodore Marvin Pollock, "The Solitary Clarinetist: A Critical Biography of Abraham Cahan, 1860–1917," Diss. Columbia 1959, and Ronald Sanders, *The Downtown Jews: Portraits of an Immigrant Generation* (New York, 1969). Both of these lengthy and detailed studies offer useful bibliographies. The most extensive bibliographies, however, are Ephim Jeshurin, *Abraham Cahan Bibliography* (New York, 1941), the only work attempting to list systematically work by and about Cahan in his three languages, Russian, Yiddish, and English (as well as a few pieces about him in Hebrew, Polish, Spanish), and the more up-to-date and useful (although it is limited to work in English) Sanford E. Marovitz and Lewis Fried, "Abraham Cahan (1860–1951): An Annotated Bibliography," *American Literary Realism, 1870–1910*, III (1970), 197–243.

Chapter One

1. Ernest Poole, "Abraham Cahan: Socialist–Journalist–Friend of the Ghetto," *The Outlook*, 99 (1911), p. 474. The quotation used in the title of Chapter Two also comes from this informative article.

2. "How I became a Socialist," *Worker's World* (Chicago, 1908), repr. in *Festschrift for Ab. Cahan's 50th Birthday* (New York, 1910), pp. 77-84.

3. The following table gives a graphic illustration of the extent of this movement. From Samuel Joseph, *Jewish Immigration to the United States; From 1881 to 1910* (New York, 1914).

Decade	Total Immigrants	Jewish Immigrants	Per cent of Total
1881-1890	5,246,613	193,021	3.7
1891-1900	3,687,564	393,516	10.7
1901-1910	8,795,386	976,263	11.7
Total	17,729,563	1,562,800	8.8

4. Moses Rischin, *The Promised City: New York's Jews, 1870-1914* (Cambridge, Mass., 1962), p. 102.

5. New York, 1976.

6. Ibid., p. 102, pp. 111-112.

7. Op. cit., 171.

8. Ira Kipnis, *The American Socialist Movement, 1897-1912* (New York, 1952), Ch. II, "The Socialist Labor Party," pp. 6-24.

9. Ronald Sanders, *The Downtown Jews* (New York, 1969), pp. 148-52. I am indebted to Sanders throughout; he provides an excellent short account of the Jewish labor and radical movements and Cahan's place in them.

10. In 1896, in an article scorning the nomination of McKinley by the Republicans, Cahan maintained that the party of the Socialist Workers was "the only true party in America"; but what he chiefly rhapsodized about was the party's "spirit," not its dialectics or specific positions. "The Ninth National Convention of the Socialist Workers' Party," *Di Tsukunft*, V (Aug., 1896), pp. 1-6.

11. Kipnis, p. 25.

12. Kipnis, p. 58.

13. "Abraham Cahan and the New York *Commercial Advertiser:* A Study in Acculturation," *American Jewish Historical Society Quarterly*, 43 (Sept. 1953), pp. 10-36.

14. Justin Kaplan, *Lincoln Steffens* (New York, 1974), pp. 84-85, 88, 93.

15. *The Autobiography of Lincoln Steffens* (New York, 1931), p. 317.

16. Rischin, p. 35.

17. Samuel Niger, "Yiddish Culture," *The Jewish People Past and Present*, IV (New York, 1955), p. 274.

18. Howe, p. 111.

19. Poole, pp. 476-477.

20. "The Solitary Clarinetist," p. 334.

21. A. Liessen, "Note to Poem," *Festschrift . . . 50th Birthday*, p. 6; *Twentieth Century Authors*, eds. Stanley J. Kunitz and Howard Haycraft (New York, 1942), p. 4.

22. For more on Cahan's domineering and intolerant qualities in his later years see Oswald Garrison Villard, *The Disappearing Daily: Chapters in American Newspaper Evolution* (New York, 1944), p. 213; for perceptive views on Cahan's "Bonapartist exercise of will," see Irving Howe, "Becoming American," *Commentary* 49 (March 1970), pp. 88–90.
23. Oscar Handlin, *The Uprooted* (Boston, 1951), pp. 177–187.
24. Niger, op. cit., pp. 282, 285, 292, 297.
25. *The American Language* (New York, 1st ed., 1919; 4th ed., 1936), pp. 633–634. In *Bleter*, III, pp. 283–285, Cahan cites the use of "Yiddishe Yiddish" (i.e., the spoken language of the unschooled masses, which was "plain" and frequently incorporated American-English words) as a chief reason for the *Forward's* success. See also Robert E. Park, *The Immigrant Press and its Control* (New York, 1922), pp. 97–107, for Cahan's insistence upon using the Yiddish language (in the way that he did) as a means of reaching the people and, in effect, convincing them the *Forward* was *their* paper.

    There is a further question related to language that has to do with Cahan's literary career: was Yiddish an appropriate vehicle for belleslettres? For Cahan, aspirations in that direction meant inevitably writing in English. This subject will be treated more fully in Chapter Three.
26. *American Judaism* (Chicago, 1957), p. 68.
27. See "Ghetto's Grief; Mourning for Dreyfus," *Harper's Weekly*, 43 (Sept. 1899), p. 947; "The Russian Jews in America," *Atlantic*, 82 (1898), pp. 128–139; "Russian Revolutionists," *World's Work*, 8 (1904), pp. 5311–15.

Chapter Two

1. For the discussion of Realism that follows I am indebted to these standard works: Walter Blair, et al., eds., *The Literature of the United States*, II (Chicago, 1966, 3rd ed.), pp. 2–44; Norman Foerster, ed., *American Poetry and Prose* (Boston, 1957, 4th ed.) pp. 941–956; Robert E. Spiller, et al, eds., *Literary History of the United States* (New York, 1960, rev. ed.) pp. 878–898.
2. Larzer Ziff, *The American 1890s: Life and Times of a Lost Generation* (New York, 1968), p. 48.
3. Foerster, p. 946.
4. Jacob A. Riis, *How the Other Half Lives* (New York, repr. 1957), pp. 92, 94.
5. Robert Hunter, *Poverty* (New York, 1904; repr. 1965); John Spargo, *The Bitter Cry of the Children* (New York, 1906; repr. New York, 1969).
6. On this subject, see the excellent article by Paul S. Boyer, "*In His Steps*: A Reappraisal," *American Quarterly* XXIII, 1 (Spring, 1971), pp. 60–78.

7. *The Popular Book: A History of America's Literary Taste* (Berkeley, 1963), 183, pp. 311–312.
8. Hart, ch. 12; and Edward Ifkovic, "The Popular Novel, 1893–1913," Diss. University of Massachusetts 1972.
9. Hart, p. 186.
10. Sanders, p. 183.
11. Ibid.
12. Sanders, p. 185.

Chapter Three

1. The story was published in book form shortly after its periodical appearance, going through several editions and enlargements—the sixth and final one in 1917. The 1907 edition used here (New York: B. Weinstein) is probably the definitive one, closest to the periodical publication. A Russian edition of *Rafael Naarizokh*, according to Cahan, provided many Jewish Socialists abroad with their most graphic portrait of life in America.
2. *The Imported Bridegroom and Other Stories* (Boston and New York, 1898). All references are to this edition. A useful reprint, *Yekl and The Imported Bridegroom and Other Stories* (New York, 1970), is unfortunately out of print at the time of writing.

Chapter Four

1. New York, 1896. All references in the text are to this edition.
2. Rudolf and Clara M. Kirk, "Abraham Cahan and William Dean Howells: The Story of a Friendship," *American Jewish Historical Quarterly*, 52 (Sept. 1962), pp. 25–57, is the best study of this subject, to which I am indebted for much of the following discussion. Howells' review of *Yekl* can be conveniently consulted in the appendix to this article.
3. William Dean Howells, *Literature and Life* (New York, 1902), p. 182.
4. Sanford Marovitz, "Howells and the Ghetto: The Mystery of Misery," *Modern Fiction Studies*, 16 (1970), p. 362.
5. *The Achievement of William Dean Howells: A Reinterpretation* (Princeton, 1968), esp. Ch. III, pp. 96–143.
6. Op. cit., p. 45.
7. (New York, 1905; repr. Bloomington, Ind. and London, 1968), p. 138.
8. Introduction to *The Rise of David Levinsky* (New York, 1960).

Chapter Five

1. 82 (July 1898), pp. 128–139.

Chapter Six

1. A collection of these stories would make them usefully available—perhaps as part of a one-volume edition of all of Cahan's stories.

Chapter Seven

1. See fn. 1, ch. 5, as well as "The Younger Russian Writers," *Forum* (Sept. 1899), and "Zangwill's Play: The Children of the Ghetto," *Forum* (Dec. 1899).
2. *Neshomah Yeseroh—Fanny's Khasonim* (New York, 1913). All references are to this as yet untranslated text.

Chapter Eight

1. Sanders, p. 344.
2. "Jewish Massacres and the Revolutionary Movement in Russia," 179 (July, 1903), pp. 49-62.

Chapter Nine

1. Isaac Metzker, ed., *A Bintel Brief* (New York, 1971), pp. 118-119.
2. In his excellent introduction to the 1960 reprint of *The Rise of David Levinsky.*
3. Interpretation of the meaning of *The Rise of David Levinsky* and assessment of its significance, as with many important books, have varied almost from the first reviews. Nathanael Buchwald in his article on "Yiddish" in the *Cambridge History of American Literature* (Vol. IV) gives it the highest praise as "a better reflection of Jewish life in American surroundings than all American-Yiddish fiction put together . . . a monumental work, and surely the most remarkable contribution by an immigrant to the American novel" (Cambridge, 1921, pp. 598-609). In *The Oxford Companion to American Literature* James D. Hart calls it "America's greatest Yiddish novel" (New York, 1956, p. 109), which it is, except that it was written in English (a translation in Yiddish did subsequently appear). There have been notably perceptive and favorable evaluations of the book, by John Macy when it first appeared, and more than a quarter of a century later by Isaac Rosenfeld and Leslie Fiedler (see annotated Secondary Sources). There are other critics who have found it undistinguished, or a libel upon Jews, or an apology for predatory capitalism, or simply unsavory. Howells wondered why Cahan, "a good man" capable of *Yekl*, was so "sensual in facts" in this book (*Life and Letters*, Mildred Howells, ed., 2 vols. [New York, 1928], p. 375).

SELECTED BIBLIOGRAPHY

Primary Sources

1. Novels in English

The Rise of David Levinsky, New York; Harper, 1917. 530 pp. Repr. Harper, 1960. Introd. John Higham.

The White Terror and the Red: A Novel of Revolutionary Russia. New York: A.S. Barnes & Co., 1905. 430 pp.

Yekl: A Tale of the New York Ghetto. D. Appleton and Co., 1896. 190pp. Repr. *Yekl & The Imported Bridegroom and Other Stories of the New York Ghetto.* New York: Dover, 1970.

2. Stories in English:

"The Apostate of Chego-Chegg." *Century,* 59, 1899, pp. 94–105.

"The Daughter of Avrom Leib." *Cosmopolitan,* 29, 1900, pp. 53–64.

"Dumitru and Sigrid." *Cosmopolitan,* 30, 1901, pp. 493–501.

The Imported Bridegroom and Other Stories of the New York Ghetto. New York, Houghton Mifflin & Co., 1898. repr. New York: Garrett, 1968, 256 pp. (A Collection of Five Stories): "The Imported Bridegroom," pp. 1–121; "A Providential Match," pp. 122–165 (appeared orig. in *Short Stories,* XVIII, Feb. 1895, pp. 191–213); "A Sweat Shop Romance," pp. 166–191 (appeared orig. as "In the Sweat Shop," *Short Stories* XIX, June, 1895, pp. 129–143); "Circumstances," pp. 192–227 (orig. in *Cosmopolitan* 22, 1897, pp. 628–640); "A Ghetto Wedding," pp. 228–256 (orig. in *Atlantic* 81m 1898, pp. 265–273).

"A Marriage by Proxy: A Story of the City." *Everybody's,* 3, 1900, pp. 569–575.

"Rabbi Eliezer's Christmas." *Scribner's,* 26, 1899, pp. 661–668.
"Tzinchadzi of the Catskills." *Atlantic,* 88, 1901, pp. 221–226.

3. Fiction in Yiddish:

"Fanny's Khasonim." ("Fanny's Suitors"). N.p., n.d. (see below).
"Mottke Arbel." *Arbeiter Tseitung,* 1841–1892. Reworked into English
as "A Providential Match" (see above).
"Neshomah Yeseroh." ("The Transcendent Spirit") *Jewish Daily Forward,*
1900–1901. Repr. New York: Forward Association (?), 1913 (?), with
"Fanny's Khasonim" (see above). 211 pp.
"Rafael Naarizokh Iz Gevoren a Sozialist" (Rafael Naarizokh Becomes A
Socialist"). *Arbeiter Tseitung,* 1895–96. Repr. New York: Yiddish Sec-
tion, Socialist Workers' Party, 1896. 80 pp., 2nd ed. *Rafael Naarizokh:
An Erzaylung Vegn a Stolyer Vos Iz Gekommen Zum Saykhl (Rafael
Naarizokh: A Story of a Carpenter Who Came to His Senses).* New
York: B. Weinstein, (?), 1907. 206 pp.
"Di Tswei Shidokhim" ("The Two Suitors"). *Arbeiter Tseitung* 1895.
(Pseud. Sotsius).

4. Articles in English: (A small selection of Cahan's work in Yiddish in
these areas is represented in the text and the Notes and References.)

Criticism and Reviews:

"I. Zangwill's 'The Grey Wig.' " *Bookman,* 17, May 1903, pp. 256–257.
"The Mantle of Tolstoy." *Bookman,* 16, Dec. 1902, pp. 328–333.
"Maxim Gorki's 'The Spy.' " *Bookman,* 29, Mar. 1909, pp. 90–92.
"Realism." *Workingmen's Advocate,* 15 Mar. 1889.
"Younger Russian Writers." *Forum,* 28 Sep. 1899, pp. 119–128.
"Zangwill's Play, 'The Children of the Ghetto.' " *Forum,* 28, Dec. 1899,
pp. 503–512.

Public Affairs:

"The Dawn of Russia." *North American Review,* 183, 5 Oct. 1906, pp.
668–671.
"Ghetto's Grief; Mourning for Dreyfus." *Harper's Weekly,* 43, 23 Sep.
1899, p. 947.
"Jewish Massacres and the Revolutionary Movement in Russia." *North
American Review,* 177, Jul. 1903, pp. 49–62.
"The Late Rabbi Joseph, Hebrew Patriarch of New York." *Review of Re-
views* (NY), 26, Sep. 1902, pp. 311–314.
"Life Begins at Eighty!" *American Mercury,* 48, Oct. 1939, pp. 221–222.
"Living Landmarks of the Russian Revolution." *Harper's,* 135, Jun. 1917,
pp. 47–55.
"Prince Kropotkin, Revolutionist." *Nation,* 112, 9 Feb. 1921, p. 201.
"The Russian Jew in America." *Atlantic,* 82, Jul. 1898, pp. 128–139.

"Russian Nihilism of To-day." *Forum*, 31, Jun. 1901, pp. 413–422.
"The Russian Revolutionists." *World's Work*, 8, Sep. 1904, pp. 5311–15.
"Stolypin and the New Terror." *Harper's Weekly*, 55, 14 Oct. 1911, p. 11.
"The Turmoil in Russia." *World's Work*, 9, Apr. 1905, pp. 6018–34.

5. Miscellaneous

English:

A Bintel Brief. Isaac Metzker, ed. New York: Ballantine Books, 1972.
Hear the Other Side: A Symposium of Democratic Socialist Opinion, Abraham Cahan, ed. with intro. New York: n.p., 1934.
Socialism Fascism Communism. Shaplen, Joseph and David Shub, eds. Intro. by Abraham Cahan. New York: American League for Democratic Socialism, 1934.

Yiddish:

Historia fun di Fareinigte Shtaaten ("History of the United States"), two vols. New York: Forward Publishing Co., 1910, 1912.
Palestina ("Palestine"). New York: Forward Publishing Association, 1934.
Rashel: A Biografia ("Raschell: A Biography"). New York: Forward Publishing Association, 1938.

Secondary Sources
Additional works are cited in the Notes and References. Reviews of Cahan's work not here cited may be conveniently referred to in Marovitz' and Fried's annotated bibliography.

1. Bibliographies and Biographies

Jeshurin, Ephim. *Abraham Cahan Bibliography.* New York, 1941, and same author, ed. *Der Vilner; Dedicated to Abraham Cahan's 80th Birthday.* New York; United Vilner Relief Committee, 1941. The only bibliography listing work by and about Cahan in Russian and Yiddish as well as in English. *Der Vilner* contains appreciative essays by Jewish writers and comrades as well. A companion volume is Spivak, Haim, ed., *Festschrift for Ab. Cahan's 50th Birthday.* New York: Jubilee Committee, 1910. Contains reminiscences in Yiddish (two greetings in English from comrades), poems by A. Liessen and Morris Rosenfeld, a translation of Howell's review of *Yekl* and other interesting material.
Marovitz, Sanford E. and Lewis Fried, "Abraham Cahan (1860–1951): An Annotated Bibliography," *American Literary Realism 1870–1910,* III, 3, Summer, 1970, pp. 197–243. The most thorough and indispensable bibliography yet to appear of work in English. Most useful annotations.
Pollock, Theodore Marvin. "The Solitary Clarinetist: A Critical Biography of Abraham Cahan, 1860–1917." Diss. Columbia University 1959.

Painstaking, detailed study. Relies heavily on Cahan's autobiography and close reading of texts.

Sanders, Ronald. *The Downtown Jews: Portraits of an Immigrant Generation.* New York: Harper & Row, 1969. The book is misnamed: it is largely about Abraham Cahan and his milieu—and it is very readable. It is especially good in its discussion of radical infighting in the labor movement and on the *Forward.*

Stein, Leon, Abraham P. Conan and Lynn Davison, trans. *The Education of Abraham Cahan.* Philadelphia: Jewish Publication Society of America, 1969. A translation of the first two volumes of *Bleter fun Mein Leben (Pages from My Life),* Cahan's five-volume autobiography (New York: The Forward Association, 1926–1931), which is the principal source for all work on Cahan. The first two volumes in Yiddish are called "In The Old Home," and "My First Eight Years in America," which in this volume become "The Old Country" and "The Golden Land." The forthcoming volume, which will complete the translation of this important American autobiography, will be called *The Rise of Abraham Cahan.*

2. Books, Articles, Reviews

Fiedler, Leslie. "Genesis: The American-Jewish Novel Through The Twenties." *Midstream,* 4, Summer, 1958, pp. 21–33. Reprinted as part of *The Jew in The American Novel,* New York: Herzl Institute Pamphlet No. 10, 1959—the best short treatment of the subject. Levinsky's failed love affairs are real failures "of a Jew in love with love and money." Cahan's ultimate subject is "the loneliness of the emancipated Jew, who has lost the shared alienation of the ghetto to become a self-declared citizen of a world which rejects even as it rewards him."

Handlin, Oscar. *The Uprooted: The Epic Story of The Great Migrations That Made The American People.* Boston: Little, Brown, 1951. Indispensable background of immigration, told in human terms, as adjustments to the new environment were required.

Hapgood, Hutchins. *The Spirit of The Ghetto.* New York: Funk and Wagnalls, 1902. Repr. Cambridge, Mass.: Harvard University Press, 1967. Introduction to reprint by Moses Rischin places Hapgood in his social context. A chapter called "A Novelist," is about Cahan (and his literary realism), who was his guide to the East Side. Perceptive reading of Cahan's stories.

Harap, Louis. *The Image of the Jew in American Literature: From Early Republic to Mass Immigration,* Philadelphia; The Jewish Publication Society of America, 1974. The first full, systematic and laudable treatment of the subject. Concludes with a long discussion of Cahan which attempts a balanced view of his work but underestimates Cahan's sophistication and insists too much on the identification of Levinsky with Cahan.

Howe, Irving. "Becoming American," *Commentary*, 49, Mar. 1970, pp. 88–90. Favorable review of *The Education of Abraham Cahan* and *The Downtown Jews.* Shrewd observations on Cahan's position as mediator between intellectuals and the masses, and on the "film of irritation" that exists in *David Levinsky*, and perhaps Cahan himself.

Howe, Irving. *World of Our Fathers: The Journey of the East European Jews to America and the Life They Found and Made.* New York: Harcourt Brace Jovanovich, 1976. A wonderful book in every way that appeared as this manuscript was being completed. Excellent on Jewish radicalism and labor, Yiddish literature and theatre, and Cahan.

Howells, William Dean. *Literature and Life.* New York: Harper & Row, 1902. As part of an article written for an English audience, Howells praises Cahan's first two books. They combine the artistic qualities of Slav and Jew and though Cahan is a Socialist he is not tendentious; lists him among writers making New York a great literary center.

Howells, William Dean. "New York Low Life in Fiction," *New York World*, 26 July 1896. Famous review of *Yekl* and Crane's *George's Mother.* Sub-heading "The Great Novelist Hails Abraham Cahan, the author of "Yekl," as a New Star of Realism, and Says That He and Stephen Crane Have Drawn The Truest Pictures of East Side Life."

Kirk, Rudolf, and Clara M. " Abraham Cahan and William Dean Howells: The Story of a Friendship," *American Jewish Historical Quarterly*, 52, Sep. 1962, pp. 25–57. Detailed and invaluable. Contains three important items in appendices: a sketch of Cahan's early life from the *Boston Sunday Post*, 27 Sep. 1896; Howells' review of *Yekl;* a translation of Cahan's tribute to Howells, *Forward*, 16 May 1920.

Macy, John. "The Story of a Failure," *Dial*, 63, 22 Nov. 1917, pp. 521–523. The best contemporary review of *Levinsky*. High praise for Cahan as an artist; perceptive about Levinsky's "triumphant failure."

Marovitz, Sanford E. "The Lonely New Americans of Abraham Cahan," *American Quarterly*, 20, Summer 1968, 196–210. A careful and rewarding study showing that the despair of many of Cahan's immigrants stems from an inner flaw or weakness rather than from the corrupting influence of America.

Maurice, Arthur Bartlett. "New York in Fiction," *Bookman*, Sep. 1899, pp. 33–49. Repr. Port Washington, New York: Ira J. Friedman, 1969. Identifies places and houses (three photographs included) serving as scenes in *Yekl*, "The Imported Bridegroom," "Circumstances," "A Ghetto Wedding." Shows Cahan as an author in the mainstream of his time.

Park, Robert E. *The Immigrant Press and Its Control.* New York: Harper, 1922. Good discussion of Cahan's early career in Yiddish journalism, and the use of a people's Yiddish on the *Forward*.

Poole, Ernest. "Abraham Cahan: Socialist-Journalist-Friend of the Ghetto." *Outlook*, 99, 28 Oct. 1911, pp. 467–478. An appreciative and in-

formative essay, by the author of *The Harbor*, going over the details of
Cahan's life and discussing his commitment to Realism in literature.

Rischin, Moses. "Abraham Cahan and the New York *Commercial Advertiser:* A Study in Acculturation," *Publication of the American Jewish
Historical Society*, 43, Sep. 1953, pp. 10–36. An excellent and detailed
account of this crucial experience.

Rischin, Moses. *The Promised City: New York Jews, 1870–1914*. Cambridge, Mass.: Harvard University Press, 1962. The basic historical study
of the subject, essential to seeing Cahan in his time and place.

Rosenfeld, Isaac. "America, Land of the Sad Millionaire," *Commentary*,
14 Aug. 1952, pp. 131–135. A sensitive and stimulating essay, one of
the best on *Levinsky*, which he sees as "an American novel par excellence in the very center of the Jewish genre."

Steffens, Lincoln. *The Autobiography of Lincoln Steffens*. New York: Har-
Harcourt, Brace, 1931. Reports with color and dash upon Cahan's presence in and effect upon the offices of the *Commercial Advertiser*.

Teller, Judd L. *Strangers and Natives: The Evolution of The American Jew
from 1921 to The Present*. New York: Delacorte, 1968. Cahan's influence upon the *Forward*, his evolving attitude towards Palestine, his
growing imperiousness, his anti-Communism.

Villard, Oswald Garrison. *Some Newspapers and Newspaper-Men*. New
York: Knopf, 1923. Contains a chapter on the *Forward*, which he
thinks "outshines" all other New York journals. Praises Cahan's role
and his efforts at popularizing through using the language of the people,
though he decries the use of sensationalism.

Library of Congress Cataloging in Publication Data

Chametzky, Jules.

From the ghetto.

Bibliography: p.

Includes index.

1. Cahan, Abraham, 1860–1951. —Criticism and
interpretation. 2. Jews in literature. I. Title.

PS3505.A254Z6 839'.09'33 76–25047

ISBN 0–87023–225–8